LEILAH PUBLICATIONS

E.A. KOETTING
EVOKING ETERNITY:
FORBIDDEN EVOCATIONS: CHTHONIAN EDITION

To order wholesale, please contact:
American Wholesale Book Company (205) 956-4151
Ingram Book Company (800) 937-8000
Baker & Taylor (800) 775-1100

Leilah Publications
P.O. Box 1863 Tempe, AZ 85280 U.S.A.
Telephone 480.239.0397

Leilah Publications LLC is an underground publishing company producing & investing in cutting edge, avante-garde artists, writers, musicians, and entertainers. We publish unconventional media that breaks all conceptual boundaries between the mystical..macabre..and the erotic. Our artistic material explores the boundaries of human consciousness, psychology, and sexuality by using literature, poetry, music, art, the occult, and theatre. Leilah Publications is a publishing company for the 21st century, not the 20th.

1

E.A. KOETTING

EVOKING ETERNITY:
FORBIDDEN EVOCATIONS:
CHTHONIAN EDITION

Illustrations

Table of Contents

Part I: The Summoning

Part II: Aided Ascent

Part I – The Summoning

When the first priests would call upon their various gods for protection or empowerment, it was rare for Ishtar or YHWY to descend from the heavens and intervene. Instead, emissaries of that deity would manifest and begin to work in the priest's behalf. Some of these early holy men would graciously accept the Divine assistance. Others would look and wonder how they themselves may possess that power: to command legions of spiritual servants armed with the ability to make the desires of their Superior manifest. If the angels can be commanded by God to turn oceans to blood, cities to ash, and people to salt, how then can I command them to do *my* will? Likewise, if the Gods of Darkness can send devils and demons forth to baptize the earth in blood and fire, what alliances would lend their obedience to *me*?

Long before the scientific invention of antibiotics, immunizations, and beautiful Latin names for every hideous malady of the body, mind, or heart of man, illness was a demon inhabiting the vessel and turning it to decay. Either the demon had to be exorcised or it would take its sacrifice. Doctors of the day would offer water, broths, herbs, and prayers to deliver the afflicted out of the clutch of the inner adversary. When the demons would leave, they would do so with shrieking violence, often their reported departure causing more suffering to their host than was suffered during the possession. Most would look on with pity, while a few would witness the event with envy.

Man has gained the knowledge necessary for him to bring legions of entities under his command, and through the endeavors of those Sorcerers not chained by fear of God or the devil, the art has been perfected. The demon can be called into full manifestation before the Evocator, materializing on this plane in a solid, beholdable form. The archangels may be called to ride their chariots and their flaming wheels into the Temple to receive their commands, and return to span their luminous wings across the heavens and bring

E.A. Koetting

about the specific apocalypse of the Magician's desire. The Black Magician may discover any spiritual being whose name has ever been called, and call him again to return to earth and to do his will. As God does, the Evocator may send forth his armies to destroy his enemies, to turn the sun to sackcloth, and to bring to world to his feet.

The earliest instances of evocation in history are seen in the warring practices of Sumerian and Phoenician empires, in which an amusing illustration of the difference between *evocation* and *invocation* occurs. In modern times and terms, "invocation" is used when an occultist or religionist calls *into* herself an amount of the power, intelligence, grace, or other qualities of a specific deity, Sephirotic sphere, or influence. "Evocation" has been used for a good deal of the history of the occult to denote the uniquely occult art of calling entities *forth*, rather than within, so that they may be communicated with in the same manner that the Sorcerer would communicate with another person of flesh. Eight to ten thousand years ago, the first cities were built and fortified with enormous walls and ornate gateways, and the Gods of its inhabitants were called within the city walls with rituals and prayers of invocation, so that they might present themselves and protect the city from harm. Certain to overwhelm every defense used against them, the enemies of an unnamed city -which is protected by the power and influence of their planetary, elemental, or Chthonic Gods - would perform their own rituals and say their own prayers which would call the Gods, Watchers, and spirits *forth* out of the city, leaving it spiritually unprotected and ready to be stormed.

Evocation has obviously evolved through time, the past hundred years having imbued this Black Magick with a more ceremonial and Judeo-Christian appearance than ever before. Finding an authenticated grimoire, which does not mention the names of some Gods and Heroes from Christian mythology, proves to be a difficult task. Despite this tainting influence, much has been discovered and recorded concerning evocation and the perfection of that art, and today the secret knowledge that was once restricted to the elite is being revealed to all. If we are able to keep our blossoming intellects from mudding up the simple truths of summoning, communicating with, and benefiting from the legions of entities that await our call, we may find ourselves Masters over our own Destiny.

Evocation is not a mysterious untouchable thing. It is a function of the spiritual machine of existence, simultaneously relying on and working to build the connection between the individual and the whole of creation, between man and God, between what is and what could possibly be.

Chapter One
Elementary Principles of Evocation

Evocation is defined for reference in the theory and Operations given in this text as the act of calling forth to visible appearance entities whose nature is beyond ordinary human sensation, for the purposes of gaining knowledge and altering reality. Although many Practitioners insist that evocation is either a strict science or a relative art, once the most basic procedures are learned and the act of evocation is mastered it is seen to be neither science nor art, but becomes as elementary to the Evocator as reading a book or driving an automobile. The act requires basic understanding of the principles and laws that govern the Operation, which once learned are integrated into the Operator's very nature. It is rare for a person who has learned to read or to drive to lose that knowledge, and once developed; the skill rarely needs to be "brushed up on" to retain the fundamentals. The reader may learn however, to read with photographic speed or might condition himself to comprehend more complex written works and strengthen his vocabulary, just as the driver might learn to operate his vehicle safely at amazing speeds over harsh terrain or under chaotic conditions. Evocation is the same. Once the elementary principles of evocation are mastered and the science or art of it becomes instinctual, the Magician may begin to use the foundation of Evocation as a means to reach into the heavens and discover the fullness of his potential. As he becomes with each evocation and with each accomplished goal more and limitless, he finds that his power – the power he has gained through this secret study of evocation – *is* indeed without limit.

While every occult discipline will insist that the rituals developed by some grand magus or another need to be adhered to without reservation in order for the evocation to succeed, the specific Operations which they peddle have no virtue in themselves but merely provide a construct by which the few basic principles of evocation can be applied. The religious and occult systems which have developed over the last six or seven hundred years have taken the simple formulae which facilitate the summoning and manifestation of a spiritual entity on the physical plane and have each made it their own by applying Divine Names and Barbarous Words of Evocation without which the whole Operation is said to be futile.

There are Operators who dutifully employ every jot and tittle of the Working as set forth by the author of some grimoire or the founder of some Order, and some of them achieve great success in their ability to conjure to full manifestation the demon that they have called. Such successes, however, are dependant on the adherence to the elementary principles that are detailed below, which their Orthodox rituals only synthesize. The rituals of the pentagram and hexagram or the Washings and Anointings of the Temple may still be used, or they may be replaced altogether, so long as the principles by which the Operation of evocation is operated are fulfilled.

Preparatory Immersion

I first attempted to perform the ritual of demonic evocation a few days after picking up a paperback copy of the pseudo-grimoire Necronomicon.[1] My occult career up to that point consisted mainly of a few candle Magick "spells" and a great deal of conversation on the subject with those that remarkably knew even less than I did. I scanned through the pages detailing the powers of the demons and the spirits, and I knew that power could be mine. I read the Mad Arab's account of the manifestations of the black apparitions, and I wanted to see. I read particularly of the Watchers, which the book claimed to the most ancient beings in existence, watching over the race of man from the beginning, dwelling in the space between creation and oblivion. The Watcher would hear my call, and would come, I was sure.

I found a flat piece of metal to use as my ritual sword, bagged a few cups of flour to spread out the Protective Circle on the ground, gathered some indigenous sagebrush leaves and pine sap for the incense, and used a white cereal bowl as my brazier. I had everything a Master Sorcerer should need for the evocation of one of the most ancient beings in existence! With bulging backpack and desperate will, I climbed a familiar mountain cliff to a cave made of metamorphic rock that was consecrated a few months earlier as my first occult Temple.

With the flour laid out in a double concentric circle, the "incenses" heaped upon the burning bowl, my sword of command gripped in my right hand and my paperback copy of the <u>Necronomicon</u> in my left, I began the first incantation to the Watcher. The cacophonic words moved from my lips into the chilled midnight air, but did not seem to travel much farther. In fact, the sound of my voice against the silent backdrop of the night startled me, sounding so alone and unanswered. I thrust the sword into the ground as the grimoire had instructed, and allowed the night to resume its silence, waiting for some sign that I was not alone after all. None came.

Frustrated with my blatant and humiliating failure as a Black Magician, I began studying the small book with a fury in the following days and weeks. I read each page several times before continuing to the next, highlighting phrases that might offer some clue to the mystery of evocation, searching for that one sentence that would unravel it all before my watered eyes. When a name or a work was cited in the editor's introduction, I followed each arrow and began reading Crowley and Shaw as they wrote of Sumer, these masters of knowledge having uncovered more of the secret understanding than I. I began to translate each incantation by referencing others given in the text and through whatever scarce translation dictionaries I could find. I read books on the mythos and society of the ancient Sumerian people, and began to fall in love with a culture that had not seen light for thousands of years. I became possessed by the <u>Necronomicon</u> and its demons, and I started to glimpse the madness of the supposed original author.

In such a maddened, obsessed state, exhausted from my research and from the emotion that I had poured into my study, I returned to the mountain cave, spread the flour on the ground, took the sword in my hand, and began the incantation. The Watcher to whom I was calling was no longer an imagined entity that I had read about, but was a well-known personage that I had studied and come to admire. The words of the ritual no longer sounded cacophonic, but instead seemed to flow from my throat and come alive in the air. I thrust the sword into the ground at the final word of the conjuration, and waited. The wind stirred, blowing leaves and dirt into the mouth of the cave. My breath stuck in my chest like molasses as the area around me grew noticeably darker despite the full moon outside and the lamps burning within the Temple. The air around me thickened and a definite presence filled the cave. The wind continued to beat its way into the Temple, the previously still night revolting against the fact that I most certainly was not alone.

The Watcher did not materialize in a physical or even visible way, although at that time in my Magical progress I did not need it to. The spirit that I summoned had answered the call, there was no doubt in my mind, and the Path for my continued growth was clear. The first principle of evocation was met, and the success of the Operation reflected such.

In order to achieve any similitude of success in the occult, the Aspirant must immerse himself in the Work *in preparation* for the ritual, becoming a zealot intent on seeing the finger of God rather than a charlatan bent on producing the image of His face. The Magician is not to only immerse himself in the doctrine and philosophy of the system which he is attempting to utilize, but in the dogma and the faith of it, although one almost inevitably follows the other. This immersion is referred to in modern Yogic teachings as a type of spiritual synthesis, and sometimes as a subjective synthesis. Many forms of Traditional Satanism, especially those derivatives of the Order of Nine Angles, call this process of spiritual integration an "Insight Role." By involving himself in the deepest levels of a political, religious, or activist group – both within himself and within the ranks of the group – the Initiate will integrate the experience and the self-knowledge gained into his collective understanding, and thus through this personal dialectic will ascend above that which he once was. For the purposes of a single ritual Operation, however, years of devotional service to one particular religion or philosophy is superfluous and unnecessary. What *is* necessary is for the Evocator to develop a connection to the powers and the specific ritual mechanism that will be used to summon forth the desired entity. The forces, beings, authority, and devices associated with the chosen entity need to become as real to the Operator as the physical world around him and all of its governing laws.

One of the most often employed methods of achieving this personal integration into a unique and specific spiritual or philosophical paradigm is through intellectual immersion. As I did after first failing to achieve *any* result whatsoever from my first evocation of the Watcher, the Magician may study the grimoire in which the name of the spirit was found, as well as reaching into other texts to obtain information about the Summoned or the system of Magick which governs that being. Since the writings of illuminated adepts such as Dione Fortune and Israel Regardie, a movement has been growing within the occult world to merge psychology, physics, and Magick.

One such psychologist/occultist/physicist, Dr. Joseph Lisiewski, Ph.D. puts forth in his book Ceremonial Magic and the Power of Evocation:

> "A state of subjective synthesis is produced in the subconscious mind of the Practitioner by the study, understanding, comprehension, and acceptance of the theoretical material underlying any magical act... It is this subjective synthesis which enables the subconscious mind to produce the physical effects associated with magical rituals, strengthen the altered state of consciousness, and enable the spiritual entity to manifest."[2]

Dr. Lisiewski hinges the entire success of the Operation on the attainment of the state of subjective synthesis, and rightly so, as without this fundamental base the whole of the Operation is pointless, the ritual of evocation being tantamount to the prayers of the faithless uttered in vain repetition.

Other methods outside of intellectualization of the material of the matter have been found to be equally effective, although often taking a form and figure quite opposite of that posited as perfect by Lisiewski. A Practitioner of Hoodoo that I once studied under manufactured his own ritual candles, adding color dyes and scented oils specific to the ritual that he intended to perform, as well as consecrating the molten wax as it was being prepared. Preceding a Working of evocation, he would manufacture three identical candles specific to the nature of the demon, scenting and coloring the candles in alignment with the attributes of the Summoned. Once the candles were formed and cooled, the Houngan inscribed the name of the spirit to be evoked, as well as its sigil or any other characters attributed to it.

The first of the three candles would be burned over a few consecutive nights before the performance of the ritual. My mentor would sit in the darkness and light the candle, focusing upon both the burning wick and the inscriptions in the wax. He would meditate upon the evocation and upon the spirit, making a conscious effort to direct his attention not towards the goal of the Operation, but rather upon the ritual itself. He would call out to the spirit by name and would announce the day and time that the evocation would begin. The candle would be blown out and put away for the next night, often the number of nights that this preparatory meditation is performed correlating with the numerology of the spirit or its origin. Rather than using his intellect to immerse himself in the Magick of the Operation, he uses the Magick itself, treating the whole of the Working as if it is already existent and needs no convincing on his part, but rather simple involvement in it to prepare himself for the glory of the evocation. Rather than using knowledge to attain faith, he uses faith to attain knowledge.

In addition to the thorough study and intellectual immersion in the theory of Magickal Operation, Hermetic Initiates will often prepare for the evocation through an intense devotion to the energies and rulers of the Sephirotic Sphere of the entity that they are to evoke. Some will decorate their house in the colors of that sphere, as well as wearing at least one article of clothing of that color at all times, and will perform a daily devotional ceremony to that Sephiroth. Others will invoke the Godform attributed to the Original Sphere of the Summoned each successive day preceding the evocation, again the number of devotional days having numerological significance to the specific entity Summoned.

Many Magickal Adepts instruct Initiates to prepare the Temple area for the evocation at least twelve hours in advance, to help produce the same preparatory synthesis of the experience.

All of these practices, even those of a purely intellectual nature, are designed to meet the demands of the first principle of evocation, which is to immerse oneself in the Working a time before it is performed, in order to perceive the impossible as certain. In order to access pure knowledge and ability, the brain must be removed from the Operation, or at the very least deprogrammed and made to get out of its own way.

Use or Development of a Working System

Most Dabblers' first evocations are performed directly from a grimoire, the rituals and incantations either followed to the letter or as the would-be Evocator sees fit in his or her inexperienced perception. Unfortunately, there are few grimoires that contain a fully operational Magickal system that can be employed to a consistently successful end. In the majority, grimoires are written for the purpose of permanently recording the vital information needed for summoning to visible appearance specific spiritual entities, rather than for providing complete instruction in the evocation itself.

The ritual of evocation needs to be performed using a tested and proven working system. It is rare for an occultist to begin his Magickal Path with her own unique and personalized ritual system that works for her infallibly. By default, if she is to have success in the occult, she will discover a system that has been shown to work for many before her, and that she will employ for the first part of her Magickal career. As the ritualist grows in experience, knowledge, and raw occult power, she will naturally take that which she has learned from others, and adding those things to her own experiences will begin to form her own fully functional working ritual system. Until that time, however, the Evocator will need to seek out a system of evocation that *works* consistently, such as that given in the fifth chapter of this text.

Putting to work a tried occult system will not only by its nature usually fulfill the basic principles of evocation, but also will give the Aspirant a structured approach to the act of evocation, which will allow him to eventually discover a system of *his own* with which he may not only perform evocation with flawless success, but also any other Magickal Operation.

Attainment of Omnipotence

The human animal, bound by the same physical laws that cause flowers to bloom and eventually wilt, is not capable of manifesting the impossible. He cannot summon the most ancient spiritual beings to physical manifestation, he cannot communicate with those things that should not be, and he cannot call the universe to move in his behalf. Those are the acts of God. In order to perform the acts of God, therefore, man must become God.

Once again looking to the various systems which have branched off from what is commonly referred to as Hermetic evocation, or more accurately, those teachings of the Hermetic Order of the Golden Dawn, as they are those that most permeate the modern occult school, most of the actual ritual of evocation is a means to this end of omnipotence, termed quite religiously as "Divine Love." This state is referred to so often as such because of the rise of emotions resulting from the influx of such an unimaginable amount of raw, usable power. The brain cannot interpret it, the mind cannot perceive it, and the body cannot contain it. Tears form at its majesty and the human that is quickly dying within the ritual is humbled by the presence of the God that is being born.

Without this "Divine love," or as is perhaps more appropriate to the Evocator desiring power for himself (as all who seek this Magick indeed do), without Divine omnipotence, no Magick can be done. The Magician will first draw, trace, or sometimes simply imagine a circle on the ground, which represents Eternity. Standing within the Circle throughout the ritual, the Magician is said to be standing "within Eternity," or within the Eternal. The actual ritualization begins after the candles have been lit, the Circle drawn on the ground, the censer coals burning red, the ritual robes donned, and all of the other pretty flashing dances are finished, with one of the most well-known and misused Hermetic rituals, the Lesser Banishing Ritual of the Pentagram.[3] Through this initial "setting apart" of the ritual space, particularly the Circle inscribed on the ground, the Magician surrounds himself with a chest-level astral ring of protection and empowerment, which will appear to his spiritual sight as a fiery blue ring floating three or more feet off of the ground. In the process of putting this astral ring into position, the Evocator

15

draws at each cardinal point a similarly flaming blue pentagram, and after each one is drawn in the air with the ritual dagger he vocally vibrates the name of the archangel attributed to that cardinal corner: Raphael to the east, Michael to the south, Gabriel to the west, and Auriel to the north. None of these archangels is actually called *forth*, but are merely called *upon*. The Magician ends the ritual by making the sign of the cross over his body and giving an oration in the Hebrew language. The Lesser Banishing Ritual of the Pentagram is used to banish any forces or entities that initially might be lingering around the Temple, and it also establishes an astral Circle of Eternity as discussed earlier.

While traditionally the Lesser Banishing Ritual of the Pentagram is to be immediately followed by a similar banishing and centering ritual, the Lesser Banishing Ritual of the Hexagram, the latter is often omitted by modern "adherents" to Hermetic or Thelemic discipline. After any and all energies and forces are chased from the Temple and the Magician stands within the Circle of Divinity, he still must perform the Middle Pillar ritual to induce the necessary Divine Love. The rite of the Middle Pillar consists mainly of visualizations that pull Divine Light into the Operator from Above in the appearance of a column of light. The Light is brought into the body through the crown of the head, and is then passed to four energy centers in the Magician's body, creating the image of a pillar of light coming down from above and running through the Evocator, who is thus armed with the "Power of God" and is hopefully, after all of this, filled with the Divine Love that is the catalyst for all Greater Works. Yet the Magician *still* must saturate the Temple and himself even more with a perceptible amount of this evanescent and seemingly incapturable Divine Love through the Supreme Invoking Ritual of the Pentagram, or Israel Regardie's suggested replacement ritual, the Opening by Watchtower. Both of these Workings consecrate the entire area for the evocation as well as open gateways through which the Divine Love may travel into this world.

All of the gestures and vibrated words of power, all of the pentagrams and the hexagrams, all of the gossamer air tracings serve to meet this one principle of the attainment of omnipotence. The same effect is desired when the devoted Practitioner fasts for days before the evocation, prostrates himself before God in prayer, and begs and pleads for the ability to do this Work, if and only if, of course, it is His will. Through the ritual or religious gymnastics, the

Operator will hopefully find himself in a state of being where he KNOWS – not feels or supposes – but knows without reservation that in that moment he is the center of existence, radiating the power of the Eternal creator and destroyer of worlds, filled with a force that cannot be smothered by all of the darkness of the abyss. In that moment, when he makes his commands, he knows that the whole of the universe becomes silent so that it may listen and obey.

Substantial Contact

Existence is bustling with entities, from insects to archangels, and the seemingly empty spaces around us may very well be constantly occupied. Any of the invisible entities may be brought into form before us, but rare is the case that just any will do. The Evocator will commonly search the grimoires and occult encyclopedias that he has collected through his career for the single spirit that can assist him in his specific goal. Often he will have several choices, but with more precise goals he will often spend quite some time poring through these tomes to find but one single entity that can manifest his will. Once the spirit has been found, its powers and abilities have been discovered, and its name has been revealed, the Summoner must make substantial contact with it in the ritual of evocation, in order to summon for certain that one spirit and no other.

While simply calling the name of most entities will cause an automatic psychic connection to establish itself, what is needed to facilitate the evocation and full materialization of the entity is *substantial contact* with the desired entity. This contact is sensed and is recognized almost invariably when it is made, and is often described as an indigo ray of light that tethers the spiritual body of the Evocator to the naturally ethereal body of the spirit. It is by virtue of this invisible or metaphoric beam of light that the spirit can travel through space and through planes from any location at any place to appear before the Magician. It is also surmised that this same connection is what allows the spirit to take beholdable form, using the ectoplasm or Prana of the Summoner to materialize a body on the physical plane.

This substantial connection is established in the evocation ritual through the devices of direct symbolism, or symbolic representations that link the mind and energies of the Sorcerer to the spirit that he is calling, rather than simply invoking or creating a sympathetic flow to a general energy pool or collective archetype. In hoodoo, this is done by using a multitude of symbols – rattles, serpents, decorative mandalas, specific food or drink, photographs, etc. – that work cooperatively to make the spiritual connection. In Western Tradition, as well as in some ancient "pagan" civilizations, this has been done through the use of a sigil.

A sigil is a drawn or engraved symbol specific to the entity to be Summoned, and is usually intricate and unique enough to avoid any two entities laying claim to the same sigil. The bulk of sigils found in traditional and modern grimoires are created through a system of mapping wherein a lamen or numerological square containing multiple letters, numbers, or figures which together represent the wholeness of the given system of Magick, is used as a consistent and unchanging base upon which the Evocator will draw lines from each letter of the spirit's name to the next. The first letter of the spirit's name is usually marked with a perpendicular line, and the last letter is marked with a loop or a circle.

The more rare type of sigil, and also the most naturally potent, is that which has been given to the Magician directly by the spirit itself. This supernatural task is usually accomplished by gaining a "mundane" psychic connection with the entity through channeling, intuitive communication, or any other means outside of physical evocation. Even rarer among this rare sigil type is the sigil drawn by the hand of the spirit itself. Putting aside both Marlowe and Disney, there is a definite reality to the manifestation of the spirit in evocation, and while in the physical, although ephemeral body that it is able to materialize the spirit may leave a similarly tangible footprint on this world, or in this case, a signature. If the Evocator places a piece of parchment in the area which the entity occupies, usually the Triangle of Manifestation, it will imprint its signature thereon when asked, or will give a sigil more personal and potent which may be used to summon it forth in the future, or will even give the sigils of its familiars which the Magician may evoke. As these signatures are astral impressions, they will fade shortly after the material form of the spirit dissipates, and must be traced over while the spiritual sight of the Evocator is still peaked and while he can still see its trace on the paper.

Rarely will ideomotor methods such as Ouija or automatic writing produce a sigil that will hold the test of time or stand its ground for the use of evocation, and is unlikely to originate from the supposed spirit even in question, but rather is fathered by the subconscious mind and its own desires.

Incantation

To create the universes, God speaks. To destroy them, he whispers. Commands spoken aloud by the Evocator, once he has attained the necessary state of omnipotence, are as commands spoken by that Eternal Source of all things often misrepresented as "God." It is not enough to close your eyes and merely think a command "really hard," to make the planets align to your will. You must command creation to bring you what you desire, with the fullness of your authority and power. Your voice needs to vibrate through the galaxies so that every molecule in existence will know that you have spoken, and that you must be obeyed.

In occult ritual, verbal commands are almost always given in the form of an incantation or a conjuration. An incantation is a sentence, phrase, or even a short monologue that is used to call physical reality into cooperation with your will. Incantations usually possess a rhythm, producing a singsong effect when it is spoken aloud. The cantor may find himself rocking or swaying with the natural rhythm produced – a motion that continues throughout his being until the force that sways him is pushed from his body and fills the area surrounding him. In contrast, a conjuration is a declarative command that specific forces or entities present themselves. The conjuration does not command action outside of the manifestation of those beings and powers summoned, but rather bring them near so that they can be commanded.

Outside of some oriental forms of mysticism, most every system of ritual and evocation provides conjurations and incantations that will bring the entity forth, call it into a visible and pleasant manifestation, and constrain it to do the will of the Evocator. Some medieval grimoires go to great lengths to successfully conjure the appropriate powers and personages, giving prayers, orations, invocations, conjurations, and multiple threats to the demon, lest he wrest himself from the Divine Command of the Magician. Almost all systems, even those that have, in their "enlightenment," broken away from the traditional Judaic or Christian terminology, call upon the names of various deities to assist in the subjugation of the Summoned.

If the Operator has met the requirements of the previous elementary principles of evocation – preparatory immersion, use or development of a working system, and attainment of omnipotence – every command issued, whether it be in the name of God or in the name of the Evocator, and whether it be the movement of a leaf or the blackening of a sun, it will be brought to pass.

Communication

All too often the Dabbler will attempt to "summon a demon" simply to see if it will "work," and he will rarely find direct success. Once the name of the demon is called within the ritual Circle, however, it will answer the Summoning, and will stand before the Magician. As the demon breathes on the Operator and its black eyes reach into his soul, the Dabbler will feel nothing. His eyes cannot see and his ears cannot hear the horror that he has called into this world.

Looking again at my above recounting of my attempted evocation of the Necronomicon's Watcher, after I had immersed myself in the Work through diligent study and honest contemplation and I returned again to the ritual and thrust the sword in the ground, the Watcher arose. As it entered this world from the ancient abyss to hear my command, and as the veil between this world and the other parted, the elements of the air began to stir. I knew that the Summoned was present, but I simply had not prepared myself to see and to hear it.

The first step in holding communication with the entity that is being evoked is to *expect* it to manifest before you. The Dabbler who is simply seeing if he can indeed summon forth a demon expects that nothing will happen, and that is what his reward is. The Neophyte who sincerely *hopes* to have contact with a being from another realm and state of existence will have little result. The Evocator who *expects* nothing less than to see and hear the Summoned, and who has prepared his senses for this unholy conversation, will experience something that will forever set him apart from those that merely wonder.

As evinced above, the second necessary component in holding conversation with the Summoned entity is to prepare the senses to be able to interpret the unimaginable. My experience in teaching the occult is that every person sees otherworldly entities all the time. Often the Seer is even aware at some conscious level that her eyes have just met with a being that they could not behold, usually through a simple sensation or intuition of the thing. Her eyes have beheld the face of an angel, but her brain is not conditioned to interpret such an experience in any usable way. Conditioning the brain to interpret these things, as is given in the fourth chapter of this text, will allow the Evocator to converse with the evoked entity with the same ease as she might talk with a friend over coffee.

A practice that had remained popular throughout the history of evocation and which has just over the last few decades been dying is to have a "medium" or a person who is indeed able to see the figures and hear the voices of the Summoned join in the ritual of evocation as an interpreter for the Magician. The Evocator would perform the rituals of invoking Divine Love and establishing an electromagnetic "buzz" in the Temple, would recite the conjuration, and when the spirit appeared, the medium would act as its mouthpiece for the Operator.

As the intellect and the self-awareness of the human race is quickening, we are finding more and more that people involved in the occult realize that they themselves *can* see and hear visitors from other realms, or can at least sense them enough to form a foundation for this Greater Sight. The young men and women who take their first steps on this Path to Power fear their own abilities less and less, and embrace their Vision and those things that they See with an openness that this world has never before known.

Issuing a Task

Issuing a task to the being that has been evoked is rarely an overlooked principle of evocation, and in fact is the one thing that most Magicians are sure to do, as the fulfillment of a specific desire is their whole purpose of learning this Art and performing the evocation. It is, nevertheless, an indispensable part of the whole act.

Once the Operator has prepared himself for the working, has reached a level of omnipotence, has spoken the incantations and conjurations which bring the entity forth, and he beholds the image of the Summoned and has communicated with it in greeting, he is to give his command. The command or charge to the spirit, whether such is for information or for action, is to be spoken with the same omnipotent authority that courses through the Operator's being, and with which he uttered the conjuration. The voice should be deepened and should come from the stomach rather than the throat, in much the same way that a baritone might sing an aria. While self-control should be maintained, keeping the Evocator from screaming or yelling, or even shriveling and whimpering at the power of the evocation, the command should be given in a clear and powerful voice. In the moment that the command is given, the Operator *must* expect nothing but the full cooperation of the Summoned. If he falls prey to the belief that the evoked entity is antagonistic to his goals, the whole of the Operation will not only fail, but will turn against him.

The wording of the command given to the spirit is equally important. For good reason, most occult instructors emphasize this function, warning that an improperly worded charge may leave far too many ways for the demon to abuse the power of the Working and harm the Magician in some way through it. While a good deal of this paranoia stems from the erroneous belief that "God" and the "Devil" are at odds with one another, and therefore angels would never assist a demonist and demons would never assist a saint, there are indeed at least a few logical reasons that the Magician will want to carefully formulate a command well in advance of the evocation.

As mentioned above, most often it is the attainment of one or a few specific goals that drives the Aspirant to pursue the secrets of evocation. As with all things, in order to achieve or accomplish anything, it must be made clear exactly what it is that you desire. Simply stating to the Goetic Duke Sallos[5] that you desire love may cause your dear aunt to send you a "thinking about you" postcard when in reality you were after sexual fulfillment. Likewise, simply telling the Duke to bring you a sexual partner might spurn some equally unwanted results. A suggested command for this type of goal would be, "Great Duke Sallos, I have summoned you here before me to bring me a young and beautiful woman to fulfill my sexual desire. As it is within your power, and as it is my will, I command that such a physically beautiful, mentally fit, and emotionally serene woman be drawn to me for the purpose of my sexual fulfillment." In addition, despite claims of karmic retribution, it may be even more advantageous for the command to direct the focus of the demon onto a single person whom you may desire.

Presenting a reasonable, yet slightly flexible timeframe for the achievement of your goal will act as a greater guarantor for its success. Although quite a few experienced Evocators have achieved spectacular results within minutes of closing the ritual, it is never a good idea to demand the unreasonable, and often improbable, of your spiritual cohort. A timeframe such as "within seven days" or "before my next mortgage payment" sets a standard of time, but also does not bind the ability of the entity with unlikelihood.

The primary reason given by the armchair and footstool theorists for carefully wording the charge to the spirit is to avoid karmic pitfalls. In the above examples of commands given to Duke Sallos, many Right Hand Path Pagans would warn that the Evocator using such charges is inviting a karmic sweep to fall upon him, by attempting to dominate the will of another soul. The Black Magician and the Adeptus Major alike have learned that necessity always dictates action.

The final quality that must be present in the command is one that is entirely unseen. The command must be made with a "wholeness of heart," all desire for the end result being transferred to the spirit when the command is given. In essence, the Operator must give up his attachment to the desire and put his trust in the evoked spirit to fulfill the command. Although this seems like a difficult leap of faith, once the entity is standing before you and your command is given as instructed in the above steps, the desire will seem to waft from your being like a tired old spirit and will no longer possess you.

Dismissal

There seems to be quite a bit of variance from system to system concerning the dismissal of the entity after it has been commanded and has agreed to its task. In the last few hundred years, it has been customary to dismiss the spirit politely and respectfully, and immediately sweep the Temple clean of its energy once its figure has dissipated.

When I began to find great success in evocation, I happened to be Working from and living in a very small apartment bedroom. I also happened to be using a form of evocation specific to the Left Hand Path and demonism. I would hang a black blanket in front of the window to block out the light, shut off the swamp cooler, and seal off the door with duct tape to contain all of the lights, scents, and perhaps even energies that were produced in the evocation.

Because of the specific evocation ritual that I was using at the time, originating from the Demonic Order to which I belonged, no banishings were to be used, as it was considered an insult to summon forth a demon to ask for its help and then to forthright banish it as an unwanted guest. I evoked the demons in the manner that was set forth by the Order, charged them to fulfill a specific task, and invited them to leave the Temple – which was my apartment bedroom – to begin their Work. As a result of this loose conclusion to the Operation, the room would remain imbued by the energies not only of the evocation, but also of the specific demons that had stood in that place.

A friend that was visiting me after a couple of weeks of daily evocation asked if I would mind turning the overhead light on. I pointed out that it was already on, and that the window was open in full daylight. His eyes widened and he was speechless, for he was sure that the darkness in the room was an absence of physical light, when in actuality it was due to the absence of *spiritual* light. After another week, my visitors would complain of a stifling atmosphere in the room, reporting a sensation of walking through fine spider webs or even through an invisible gelatin mass when they entered. Finally, when a romantic interest would constantly awaken at night unable to breathe, I realized that it might be time to clean the spiritual clutter from my apartment.

This recounting may cause many to conclude that post-evocation banishing *should* most definitely be practiced at the close of the ritual. However, the stifling spiritual blackness in my room provided an unmatched catalyst for each successive evocation, the demons manifesting much more rapidly, as well as the goals of the Working being attained with unbelievable speed and accuracy. Living in, breathing, and constantly wrapped in the invited darkness, I found myself empowered by it rather than suffocated. I was "in my element" in the darkness, and would only banish it when it began to cause physical or severe psychological harm to my visitors.

At the close of every ritual, the Summoned is to be dismissed politely, and with respect. It is customary to thank the entity for manifesting in the first place, for conversing with you, and for quickly and effectively pursuing the task that you have given.

The choice of cleaning out the Temple after dismissing the Summoned through a simple banishing or exorcism rite, however, is simply a choice that holds consequences and rewards either way. It is suggested that the individual Operator experiment and see for his or her self which provides the greatest rewards with the smallest sacrifice.

Psychological Retraction

After the evocation ritual has been completed and the spirit has been sent to accomplish the task it has been given, and after the ritual area has been banished (or has been left to absorb the energy of the Working), the Evocator must remove himself from the Temple, physically and psychically. As mentioned earlier, the human brain is not conditioned to cope with the often acausal experience of evocation, and possibly may never fully become so conditioned. The Operator's psychological and physiological states must return to their ordinary functions as naturally and smoothly as possible. This is best done by engaging in some "ordinary" behavior, where the brainwaves, breathing, and blood flow may return to normal. Making a meal, going on a relaxing walk, or even watching television are wonderful suggestions for achieving this natural return.

An effect of psychological retraction is that the whole event may seem like a distant dream, not happening <u>to</u> you, but simply witnessed <i>by</i> you. In actuality, the evocation did not happen to the person who is watching the most outrageous talk show or making a bologna sandwich. That person slept while the God that is the True Identity of the Evocator awoke and took hold of Destiny.

Chapter Two

The Summoned

Almost everyone can conjure to mind an image of a Sorcerer standing within a Circle of Protection facing a semi-transparent figure forming out of the fog or a demon engulfed in flames, holding communication and making demands. What are these beings, though, and where do they come from? From where do they get their godlike powers, and why would they share their thrones with mere mortals?

One of the greatest divisions in the schools of occult thought concerns the objective reality of entities, thus it is with that first division that the nature of the Summoned will be dissected. For the past 200 years the idea has been rapidly evolving that entities do not actually exist as their own independent beings, but instead are projections of the psyche of the Summoner in the most profound manner possible. In dealing with entities, the Magician is said to actually be dealing with himself, making pacts that only he can keep and issuing commands that his own subconscious mind will fulfill. The visions and the voices of the spirits summoned are mere hallucinations induced by massive endorphin and dopamine secretion in the brain, possibly leading to extensive neuropeptide release that could probably lead to more of the brain's unused centers being activated and working upon the outside world. The Divine Love spoken of in the previous chapter is, according to this theory, the simple euphoria produced by such adrenal secretions, and if harnessed will allow the subject (notice that the ritualist in this context can no longer be considered to be the Operator, as he is at the mercy of his own toxic state) to hold communication with his hallucinations and convince them, i.e. convince himself that he is worthy of the goals that he has set and that he can, indeed, achieve them.

Some quasi-metaphysicians attempt to reconcile this theory and the other, picking and choosing which effects are caused by internal chemistry and which are actually Divine or spiritual. For instance, it is often thought that the entities that may be evoked are not "real" aside from their existence in the Magicians "independent reality," but instead are portions of the brain which are regularly dormant and which can be brought into at least partial activity through the evocation. Such a pseudo-self-psychology is claimed, however, to bring a person nearer to the Divine, to God, or to some great, vaporous Cosmic Consciousness. Some spiritual entities and concepts exist, but some of the others most definitely don't... especially the mean and nasty ones. You must allow the chemicals of your brain to overwhelm your will in order to achieve the goal that your will dictates, rather than utilizing your will in its greatest degrees to stifle the calculating interruptions of the brain and have an honest, Magickal experience. You must be high to be spiritual, but you cannot under any circumstances be spiritual to go Higher.

The opposite school of thought is that school which seems to do most of the hands-on-training, rather than pontificating on the theories of the "power of the mind." Occam might agree that if you can see a demon's hideous face, hear its rumbling voice, smell its noxious odor, and benefit *directly* and *precisely* from its Work, that the demon was in actuality real. The adversarial philosophers might counterclaim that such an entity existed only in the mind and senses of the Operator, in strict accordance with the internal and external conditions that he had established prior to and during the ritual of evocation. They argue this, those who have never blackened the sky with storms, risen the dying from their hospital beds with the power of angels, or have witnessed demons tearing the flesh off of their enemies. There is a terrifying truth to the reality of these Works, both in their benevolence and in their evil. That truth will be revealed as the Operator operates upon this real and physical world with the spiritual creatures that wait to be called, and as he turns this key to limitless power and finds that he is the same.

Angels

Images of chubby, winged cherubs that drift on painted clouds and beautiful, maternal women in flowing white robes linger in the mind as the prime archetypes of supposed angelogy, even if such manifestations are far from reality. Although the original Latin word "angelus" literally means "messenger," it is clear even from the time of the first war in heaven spoken of in Christian Mythology that the angels do much more than deliver God's messages. Sammael brought pestilence to Egypt in the form of seven plagues. Gabriel turned the cities of Sodom and Gomorrah into a sea of sulfur and brimstone. Michael guards the swirling fiery rings of God's throne. The angels stand as warriors, waiting for their names to be called by their Lord to fly into the battlefield, armed with the might of the Eternal.

Most entities that can be classified specifically as angels and no other are found in the Judeo-Christian texts and teachings, or the occult derivatives thereof, such as Rosicrucianism and Kabbala. While a good deal of Christian sects will pray either to the angels directly for assistance or to God through Jesus' name to have the angels deployed in the parishioner's behalf, the system that is known specifically for its use of the evocation of the angels is Kabbala.

Kabbalists understand the Tree of Life as a symbolic representation of the placement of, connection between, and the importance of the major forces of the creation and sustentation of existence. The Tree of Life consists of 11 spheres, or Sephirah, which each correspond with a planetary sphere, an element, and a specific aspect of the Divine. Each Sephirah, which is in actuality a non-real symbolic construct by which metaphysicians may better understand the nature of the Eternal, host's numbers of spiritual entities whose power, knowledge, and ability directly substantiates that singular Divine quality. Usually a single archangel presides over the Sephirah, and the vibration of a specific Divine Name unlocks the energies of that sphere for the Magician.

The entities, with which we are dealing here, angels and archangels, seem to be at the head of the Sephirotic hierarchy. They are armed with the fullness of the power of their stations, being perfectly equipped to manifest the desire of the Evocator so long as his or her wishes are in alignment with the Original Intent of the angel. If the Magician is in need of healing, he may find more effective assistance from an angel of the sphere of Netzach or Hod than from Binah, not because the Saturnian entities are not willing to help, but because it is not within their specialized ability to do so.

Given below is a concordance for each Sephirah, its planetary correspondent, and the powers and abilities of the angels of each.

1.   The Sephirah of Malkuth is represented in the physical plane as earth. Its angels have power over the four elements of fire, water, earth, and air, as well as the cardinal directions of north, east, south and west, each direction and element having an individual power and purpose. While the specific elemental spirits are treated in their own category apart from the Angelic Orders and Sephiroth, the ruling angels of Malkuth are dealt with in the same manner as the angels of the remaining ten Sephirah. Malkuth is ruled over by the archangel Sandalphon.

2.   The Sephirah Yesod is represented in the physical plane as the moon that orbits the earth. Its angels have power over the initial forms of ritual Magick, witchcraft, and illusion, as well as sexuality and the minor currents of intuition. Yesod is ruled over by the archangel Gabriel.

3.   The Sephirah Hod is represented in the physical plane as the planet Mercury. The angels of Hod are given power over the sciences, especially medicine and alchemy. They are great instructors in these arts, as well as having miraculous ability to heal any malady and to adjust the elements of the lower world to provide for the spiritual Ascent of the Magician. Another ability of the angels of Hod is to assist the Evocator in discovering the secrets of Magickal Initiation, opening doors for further spiritual

growth and self-discovery, either as a solitary Practitioner or through the vehicle of a religious Order. The archangel ruling over the sphere of Hod is Michael.

4.   The Sephirah of Netzach is represented in the physical plane as the planet Venus, which has for millennia been synonymous with love and peace. Aside from their power over these invisible emotional currents, the angels of Netzach have great influence over the forces of passion, in its many forms. It was known to the Sumerians, Greeks, and Romans that the Goddess of Venus, by her many names, was both the matron of lovers and the defender of warriors. If ever the heart is fully engaged in a cause, whether that cause is for procreation or for destruction, for art or for death, the Venusian Goddess dwelled in that heart. Haniel is the archangel that rules over Netzach.

5.   The Sephirah Tiphareth is represented in the physical plane as the sun, the source of all light and abundance in our solar system. As such, the angels of Tiphareth have power over wealth, health, protection, and prosperity of all sorts. All that is good and life sustaining is governed by these angels. The archangel ruling over this Sephirah is Raphael.

6.   The Sephirah Geburah is represented in the physical plane as the planet Mars. The angels of Geburah have power over power itself, over strength and vitality. In this sphere and its inhabitant angels is held the currents of domination and victory through aggression. The archangel ruling over Geburah is Kamael.

7.   The Sephirah Chesed is represented in the physical plane as Jupiter, the largest planet in our solar system. Its angels have influence over the powers of leadership, rulership, and great affluence. Chesed is ruled over by the archangel Tzadqiel.

8.   The Sephirah Binah is represented in the physical plane as the planet Saturn. The angels of Binah possess knowledge

of the most ancient teachings and the most secret doctrines, as well as having power over death, destruction, disease, and ill fortune. It is known to some adherents and Orders of Traditional Satanism and Dark Ascent that Binah is one of the three spiritual gateways in the whole of the universe that leads into the realm of the Dark Gods, which is an acausal dimension lying deeper beneath creation than even the abyss. Binah is the realm of pure understanding, the likes of which are deathless and ageless. The archangel ruling over this dark sphere is Tzaphqiel.

9.   The Sephirah of Da'ath is often called the "invisible Sephirah," meaning that it has no corresponding planet, although modern occultists such as Zechariah Sitchin believe that it is represented by the planet Nibiru which has an orbital pattern outside of the solar orbit of the remaining planets, and which passes into our solar system every 3,600 years, bringing with its return apocalyptic maelstrom. Others of a darker influence posit that a wormhole or an actual physical gateway into another dimension exists in the space between the planets Saturn and Neptune. Other, perhaps more objective, occult philosophers relate the Sephirah to the planet Pluto. The "angels" of Da'ath are as hidden as the Sphere itself, and are said by many Kabbalists to never have common intercourse with mortals and Magicians, but serve a Higher Function for those that are ready to cross through the abyss into the realms of Godhood. Yet another view is that Da'ath is the Sephirotic Sphere linking the Sephiroth to the Qlippoth, or the Tree of Death, also called the Evil and Adverse Tree. As such, the "angels" of the sphere of Da'ath would in actuality be the Qlippothic demons. Regardless, the powers emanating from this invisible Sephirah are those of the Final Initiation of the Aspirant, the destruction of the Lower Self, which may have the end result of the absolute oblivion of the individual, or the resurrection of the God within. Spiritually and Magickally traversing through Da'ath is the end of the mortal and all of his fallible comprehension, and is the Path to the greater understanding that all is nothing. As it seems with all things relating to the sphere of Da'ath,

there is great argument concerning the archangel of the hidden Sephirah. Most traditional Kabbalists claim that since Da'ath represents the abyss, wherein nothing can dwell, there is no archangel ruling over it. In opposition is the thought that the archangel Amahiel is given reign over the powers and entities of Da'ath, while others claim that it is none other than Chorozon.

10. The Sephirah Chokmah is represented in the physical plane by the planet Neptune. The angels of this sphere have dominion over the higher faculties of intuition and seership. The word "Chokmah" is translated to English as "wisdom," and it is this non-intellectual comprehension that Chokmah's angels both contain and can cultivate in the Evocator. The archangel ruling over Chokmah is Raziel.

11. The Sephirah Kether is represented in the physical plane by the planet Uranus. The angels of Kether have dominion over the pure knowledge of Divinity, and can assist the Magician in discovering this Godliness within himself. The archangel presiding over Kether is Metatron.

Although the above Sephiroth represent the majority of angelic influences in known occult existence, there are angelic beings that seem to exist independent of the Kabbala, being passed down from traditions more ancient than the Jewish system. Most often, these angelic outsiders will become known to the Evocator through the experience of evocation itself, rather than through the study of spiritual and metaphysical philosophies. While Kabbalists will attempt to assign these angels to one Sephirah or another, it is clear to both the Magician and the angel that perhaps God has secrets that even the most elect are not privy.

When evoked, angels usually manifest as benevolent, kind, compassionate, and loving figures. They are beautiful to look upon, speak in soft and flowing voices, and rarely assume forms that are not akin to human. Archangels, conversely, are seen as large beings whose power is too great to be contained or commanded, whose purposes are too specific to be wavered, and whose intelligence is too timeless to be outwitted. Nevertheless, the Evocator will see these powerful beings acting quickly and flawlessly in his behalf, literally causing miracles to return to the earth at his command.

Demons

It would be a comforting thought that only those unenlightened, medieval-minded Christians of the western world have fallen prey to the eternal enemy dualism; unfortunately, the whole of the human race dwindles in an unwinnable ideological war between good and evil which plays itself out in every language in every sacred scripture. God and Satan and all of their armies once fought a war using spiritual spears and ethereal swords, in which Satan and his minions were flung to earth to reside until the Day of Judgment. The demons of the Christian faith still war with God through their ability to deceive His mortal children. Islam also has their well-known Jinn who seem to possess a form, mind, and will similar to human. Conversely, Hinduism offers the Asuras as the demon servants of the Black Magician, which are deities that in their hunger for power have lost the grace and reverence that would otherwise place their thrones alongside those of the Devas.

Demons are quite often portrayed in literature and art as impish, unintelligent, and weak, especially when the authors and artists have been on the church's payroll. When measured against the horrible stories that are told in Sunday school and church firesides about the demonic induced illnesses that Jesus had to cure, the latest possession and haunting movies, the historical accounts of pacts with the devil, and real-life personal experiences with demons, the classical portrayal of the imp does not seem to fit. What are the real demons like then, and where can the Magician find them?

Although the entities that are found in many of the traditional grimoires and demonological encyclopedias are a bit too easily filed away as demons and as "enemies of God," a good deal of them would otherwise be considered planetary or even Sephirotic entities, others could be identified as group or cultural egregores, while only a small minority would remain, after careful and unbiased inspection, demons.

Qlippothic demons are an obscure group of entities whose exact nature has been intentionally diminished in writing and oral tradition, yet which still seem to emerge, and the demons of which still manifest inside the Temple when the Black Magician dares to call their names. According to the Kabbala, and most other initiatory spiritual philosophies, God is the perfect mathematician and is the grand balancer of all things. Every power, province, principality and dominion must have an equal and opposite party, as well as every emotion, thought, organism, and cell, lest one thing is left alone, not having any definition without an opposite and therefore not existing to serve the purpose of its creation. Every molecule has been set in its place exactly where it should be, and always in perfect relation to its opposite. The Tree of Life, or the Sephiroth, is no exception to the Law of God, and existence is therefore presented with the perfect balance to the Kingdom of Heaven made manifest. Every Kabbalic and Judaic myth, as well as speculation that has been inserted over time, gives quite a few contradicting stories of the origin of the Qlippoth.

Typhonian Luciferianism holds to the thought that in the same manner of the creation of the Sephirotic Tree of Life, the Qlippothic Tree of Death was formed in the spiritual universe, to establish that delicate balance of opposites. Many Kabbalists consider this view to be that of unenlightened brothers of the Left Hand Path in an attempt to give Darkness a throne equal to Light, or, at best, an uninformed vantage taken by those struggling to appear educated in the esoteric mysteries of the Kabbala. The conventional explanation of, or perhaps apology for, the Qlippothic Tree is that the Sephirotic Spheres emanate a specific energy and are host to specific entities, and when one or more Sephirah is unbalanced with the others, that one Sphere will exude an uncontrolled amount of their natural potency, thus giving reign to unrestrained forces, and feeding beings whose very nature is chaos.

What *is* known to the practicing Sorcerer, however, is that the Qlippoth are habitations existing in the spiritual realms, and can be viewed in scrying or visited in state of projection or Travel. The demonic inhabitants of the Qlippothic Spheres also exist, and their adverse power is indeed the perfect balance to that of the angels.

The names of the Qlippothic Spheres are given below, along with the Sephirotic correspondent and the ruler of each sphere. Although some of the names of the Qlippoth are also the names of specific demons, such is due to the meaning of the demonic title, rather than a direct correlation between the specific demon and that sphere.

1.   Nahemoth, also called Lilith, is identified as the imbalanced Sephirah of Malkuth, and is translated as "Evil Woman." The energies and demons of the Sphere of Lilith have influence over the carnal aspects of mortals, leading them into lustful and "sinful" acts that would pull them away from spiritual Ascent and towards the state of an instinctual biped. The Evil Chief or Grand Demon of Lilith is Nahemah.

2.   Gamaliel is identified as the imbalanced Sephirah of Yesod, and is translated as "The Obscene Ones." The demons of Gamaliel further the evil work of the demons of Lilith, going beyond mere provocation to moral animalism in their power over corruption of the mind and heart. Where the angels of Yesod instill the initial sense of power and Magick in the life of the Evocator, the wicked angels of Gamaliel plant the seeds of malice. Gamaliel is, interestingly, ruled over by the Grand Demoness Lilith.

3.   Samael is identified as the imbalanced Sephirah of Hod, and is translated as "Poison of God." Where the angels of Hod teach medicine and science, the demons of Samael teach the art of reversing the health of others and forbidden alchemy of the darkening of the soul through Demonic Descent. Where the Mercurial spirits and angels guide the Magician in the sciences that bring oneness with God, it is a forbidden metallurgy and alchemy that is taught by the dark angels of Samael. The Qlippah Samael is ruled over by the Evil Chief Adramalech.

4.   A'arab Zarak is identified as the imbalanced Sephirah of Netzach, and is translated as "The Raven of Dispersion." The demons of A'arab Zarak are often seen in their manifestations as ravens with the heads of demons. Their control is ironically over lack of control. When Netzach is in perfect harmony with Hod, intelligence and passion unite to propagate harmony and to provide a continuous flow of Divine Love into the lower worlds. When they are

not balanced, A'arab Zarak, and all of its demons reign over unbridled lust, greed, and jealousy, which can result in the crimes of rape, theft, and murder. The Arch-Demon ruling over A'arab Zarak is Baal.

5. Thagerion is identified as the imbalanced Sephirah of Tiphareth, and is translated as "Painful Movers," or "Disputers." The demons of Thagerion manifest themselves as great, black giants full of anger and wrath towards even their allies. They have power over enmity, setting lovers, families, societies, nations, and even worlds against one another. They are governed by the Grand Demon Belphagor.

6. Golachab is identified as the imbalanced Sephirah of Geburah, and is translated as "The Burners with Fire." The demons of Golachab have the power of arson, making the solar light that once shone over all things in bounty to be used for bane, making red with flames all things that once were green. Golachab is ruled over by the Evil Chief Asmodeus.

7. Ga'agsheblah is identified as the imbalanced Sephirah of Chesed, and is translated as "The Disturber of All Things." Rather than presiding over creation as leaders in the manner of the angels of Chesed, the demons of Ga'agsheblah use their power and abilities to lead the universe into disarray. A greater function of these demons is to teach the Qlippoth Arts to the Black Magician, whereby he may utilize the same powers and energies as the demons, and may reign as a God of Darkness upon earth. This Sphere is governed by Astaroth.

8. Satariel is identified as the imbalanced Sephirah of Binah, and is translated as "The Concealers." The demons of Satariel are given the power of concealment, of secrecy. While this power, at first glance, may seem not only vague, but also unimpressive, in Working with Sateriel's inhabitants it quickly becomes clear that one of their greater functions is to perform and to teach the concealed

arts, or the secret arts, especially those involving the recalling of chaos and baneful Magick. These secret Operations offer the Dark Initiate some of the most potent keys to demonic power. The ruler of Sateriel is the notorious Evil Chief Lucifuge.

9. Daath is the ninth Qlippah, whose attributes are the same as given for the Sephiroth, as it is the only sphere that remains in both the Tree of Life and that of Death, connecting the two symbolic entities in the same manner that life and death, good and evil, damnation, and exaltation are inseparably connected.

10. Gagiel is identified as the imbalanced Sephirah of Chokmah, and is translated as "The Hinderers." The energies exuding from that sphere, and the power that its demons possess, bind the universe and restrict creation from fulfilling its full potential, which often takes the form in human interaction as self-delusion, confusion, consternation, and stagnation. Beelezebuth governs the Sphere of Gagiel.

11. Thaumiel is identified as the imbalanced Sephirah of Kether, and is translated as, "The Twins of God." The powers of the Sphere and its demons create a distinct bipolarity between man and God, each the other's enemy. Through this, the Lower is cut off completely from the Higher, and the Light of God is shut out from the Darkness entirely. By some sources, the ruler of Thaumiel, and therefore the Head of the whole Adverse Tree is Moloch; others give that title to Satan.

Although the Divine and Infernal Enumerations, the Sephiroth and the Qlippoth, may at present seem either superfluous or entirely meaningless, in ritual they become irreplaceable. By simply meditating upon the Hebraic name of a specific Sephiroth or Qlippoth, the energies of that Sphere will begin to flow into the life of the Operator. In advanced methods of evocation, as those given in this text, the Evocator will travel to the spiritual domains relating to each of the Sephirah and Qlippah,

Largely, the demons that occupy the various Qlippoth are not named in writing, but are to be discovered through the evocation of the Grand Demon of that Sphere, who will at that time release the names, sigils, and methods by which his inferiors may be evoked. The same seems to be true of a good number of the demons that have proven themselves to be indispensable to the practicing Black Magician or Demonist, their names written only in the personal metaphysical journals of their Evocators, the secrets of their Summoning discovered through secret methods that are being divulged, many for the first time, in this text.

A good deal of the modern belief in and fear of demons comes from a source which benefits immensely from "superstitions": the Church. Art, literature, urban legend, and even modern cinematic production have been funded by the Church in its various names and divisions, to propagate the belief that the sole concern of the demonic armies is to secure the souls of untithed parishioners and of the obviously already possessed gentiles. Unfortunately for those Aspirants seeking real knowledge and understanding of spiritual reality, the aforementioned source is the least objective and would be the first to stifle even the hint of a spiritual reality outside of their Papal reign. The demonologists and exorcists of the Catholic faith work only within their own paradigm, never reaching into the endless worlds of the occult to discover the "inside truth" of the matters which they peddle as their forte. Interesting to note is that despite the Catholic exorcists' claims of defeating the demon through their borrowed rituals, the life of the exorcist is expected to continue no more than 15 years after he begins to make enemies with demons, the Church itself citing case after case of exorcists' deaths by heart failure, stroke, or horrible "misfortune."[2] It is then the exorcist that is defeated and the demon that will continue to plague its adversaries with the same enmity that was the breath of its very creation.

Protestant "demonic deliverance ministers," seems to have the exact opposite effect. The whole efficacy of their deliverance Operations relies upon the faithful cooperation of the possessed, whereas the Catholic exorcist is able to battle the demon in spite of the retaliation of the possessed. While the Catholic exorcist's problem lies in the fact that his effective rituals, borrowed as most of that church's ceremonies are, are too effective to be wielded by an outsider to the demonic arts, the Protestant Deliverance Minister's problem lies in the complete inefficiency of the Operation, always having at hand the insurance policy of, "if only your faith is strong enough."

Although the demons listed in the pages of the Orthodox demonological texts are in the majority the created egregores or archetypes of the religion of the authors of such a text, those demons have been created all the same, and exist to serve the function of their origination, which may possibly be utilized by the Demonist. In working with the entities whose names and attributes are only found within the works and words of the various Christian churches, the Evocator will usually find the impish cohorts of the denigrated devil who are bound by the imposed laws of the spiritual and psychological system which brought them into being. The goblins of God's established "Kingdom on earth," while impotent in performing the hideous miracles of the Solomonic, Qlippothic, Chaotic, or Chthonic demons, are expert pests, and can be directed to accomplish simple feats rather quickly. In contrast to their ability to make dramatic, lasting changes in reality, the supposed Fallen Angels of the Christian faith usually possess remarkable poltergeist abilities. Much like the creators of the system that binds them, their concern is for the appearance rather than the essence.

Referencing comparative sources for information on demons, overlaps are noticed immediately. Demons that existed long before the Judaic religion was invented appear in the encyclopedias of demonology as low-ranking officials in the Infernal Hierarchy, and demons that never have had anything to do with the Christian system of religion and ritual are listed under Satan's command as well. This evidences two points: the authors and authorities of the encyclopedias in question have few if any experiences in demonism outside of their own paradigm; and the truly powerful demons that they have encountered have paid lip service to a dead messiah and his servants so that their names might forever be recorded in the annals of spiritual and religious history.

Due in a large part to the immediate availability of information, study, and research findings that we are graced with today, it has become a near religious devotion in itself by New Age authors to discredit both the original authors of demonic grimoires, and the demons themselves, by pointing out similarities between the demon in question and some deific figure of a past civilization. The most common identification between the two is through names.

In his book <u>Summoning Spirits: The Art of Magical Evocation</u>, the occult author Konstantinos makes reference to this by saying, "Throughout history, the gods of one group of people would always become the demons of their conquerors. This seems to occur in the Goetia. One of the spirits, Astaroth, is actually a thinly disguised godform of the Mesopotamian goddess Astarte."[1]

While the historical base of this statement is irrefutable, the Magickal application of it is obviously flawed. Astaroth is described in the Goetia as malicious masculine angel, and is rarely referred to in any manner of beauty, while Astarte has contrarily always been known as a beautiful and voluptuous woman. Likewise, the essence of Astarte is that of passion and love, while the powers of Astaroth seem to lie in his expert knowledge of what is often referred to in the occultic grimoires as "the liberal sciences," as well as his standing as the Grand Duke of Hell. If any perversion of her image was made, it was not in the form of this demonic ogre, but by the Egyptians in their Goddess Saosis, the Greeks in Aphrodite, and the Romans in Venus, the multi-named goddess having been passed around to seemingly every religion, including Christianity as Mother Mary. Again, using the aforementioned example of the connection between a well-known demon and a similar deity, the only possible link between the two would be a matter of simple etymology rather than genealogy.

While from the vantage of the ever-present armchair of occult teachings it may seem obvious that the Church in particular did and does endeavor to minimize the power of other civilizations and cultures through demonizing their deities, when the Black Magician evokes to full manifestation the demons listed in the pages of grimoires or encyclopedias, that demon most surely does manifest, and not a jewel-clad goddess in the nude. Theorists will then posit that the manifested demon has been created by the author of the work at hand and the collective Evocators that use that grimoire, either metaphysically through belief or psychologically through the same. Either way, the demon that is listed is the demon that arrives when his name is called, or more can be learned through that ritual interaction than a million years inside of the armchair.

Elementals

A common ritual practice in the modern Neo-Pagan teachings and subculture is to call upon the powers of the elements of fire, water, earth, and air, which are known to the Gaeaic adherents as spiritual forces which manifest themselves in diluted forms on the physical plane, but which bind the whole of the organism of nature together on the astral and higher planes.

As there exist the four distinct energies of fire, water, earth, and air, there also exist entities that sustain the balance between them and carry out the dynamic activities of their particular element. The entities of a specific element are said to have "bodies" composed of the very element itself, and they are the representatives of the finer, distinct attributes of the element. Each element can be seen as having in its charge a type of entity that is unlike any other... a creature that exists by and for that one element alone. As all prolific societies do, both above and below, the elemental entities also act within a set and unchallengeable hierarchy.

The element of fire is sustained and supported by beings that are often closely identified with the mythical descriptions of the salamander, although few manifest as anything other than human shape when evoked. They are governed by the elemental King Djin. Aside from their ability to create and manipulate the physical manifestation of fire, the Salamanders have the ability to stir up passion and lust in a person, to impart vitality and vigor, to excite rage or aggression, and to destroy obstacles in the path of the Evocator, all of which are said to be the manipulation of the finer, or astral, manifestation of fire.

The element of water is sustained and supported by beings called "Undines," or water nymphs, which appear as beautiful young women, usually bare-breasted. The Undines are governed by the elemental King Nichsa. Aside from their ability to manipulate the watery forces of nature, such as rain, snow, fog, and eventide, the Undines are able to help the Magician develop his or her emotional maturity and understanding, as well as providing basic assistance in relationship and reproductive matters. Water being a Neptunian force, Undines are powerful in their ability to also assist in the development of clairvoyant and intuitive abilities.

The element of earth is sustained and supported by beings referred to as "Gnomes," which have played a large part of Nordic and Scandinavian derived folklore as short, stocky people who usually specialize in forms of gemology. The Gnomes are governed by the elemental King Ghob. While the Gnomes are able to fortify a person with physical strength, mental stamina, and emotional surety, their power over the wealth of the earth is usually the cause for their evocation by most occultists. They have a remarkable ability to manifest abundance with great speed and to perfect specification, although they are less inclined to deliver enormous amounts of money to the Summoner than demons and some angels.

The element of air is sustained and supported by beings often called Sylphs, which are very similar in nature and description to the sprites which have appeared in literature and cinema over the last hundred years, manifesting in the ritual of evocation as beautiful, petite, winged spirits with childlike faces and soft voices. Unlike the voluptuous beauty of the Undines, the Sylphs carry an air of complete innocence with them, and are sometimes described by occult Practitioners as being playful – sometimes too much so for the liking of the serious practitioner. Nevertheless, Sylphs have proven to be the some of the most effective entities to summon when the Magician is in need of help in improving mental faculties. They have the natural ability to assist in the absorption of intellectual concepts more quickly and deeply than before, as well as giving aide in the development of the scrying vision needed for the greater Works of Magick. Most startling, however, is their power over the physical element of air, being able to manipulate it in cooperation with the element of water to create storms and hurricanes, with earth to cause tornadoes and blistering desert winds, and working alone to aide in what may seem to be levitation. The Sylphs are governed by the elemental King Paralda.

Planetary Intelligences and Spirits

In each planetary sphere, or Sephirah, there are two divisions of entities that serve beneath the angels: Planetary Intelligences and Planetary Spirits. Planetary Spirits are those entities that are given the power to act, to sustain the balances between the Sephirah, and to alter known reality in accordance with its specific function. These are the entities that the Magician would summon should he desire quick and precise change in his world. Planetary Intelligences, on the other hand, are the intellectual arm of the Sephirah, holding all of the knowledge of that sphere, guiding in counsel in accordance with the particular knowledge held by a particular Intelligence. The Evocator would therefore call upon a Planetary Intelligence if information is desired rather than direct alterations in reality.

The interesting thing about Planetary Intelligences and Spirits is, however, that their origins date much farther back than the system of Kabbala, and therefore farther back than the Tree of Life to which each spirit and intelligence corresponds. Indeed, these entities, which are thought to serve under the command of the Sephirotic angels, existed long before any religion had even considered the existence of angels. The Chaldeans and Sumerians looked at the nearby stars and began attributing the powers of spirits, energies, and even Gods to each planet, thereby creating a system upon which every religion and science would build for the remainder of human life on earth.

Planetary Intelligences and Spirits are some of the most easily evoked beings in existence, and they are always pleased to assist the Magician in whatever task he may require. These entities are extremely limited, however, in performing tasks even closely outside of their specific set powers, and may refer the Evocator to another Spirit to accomplish the goal.

Spirits of the Dead

It is a common folk belief that when outstandingly "good" people die and are risen in some heaven or another, that they are granted the standing of angels, and that through such a title they are able to watch over and protect their loved ones still on earth. This belief has been dualized through the idea that when outstandingly evil people die, they reawaken in this world in a spirit body, by which they can haunt and torment the living, trying desperately to continue their wicked reign from beyond the grave. Somewhere in the middle are those who themselves were tormented in life, either living a tortured existence, or dying a tragic death. In some instances, these victim souls are seeking the help of the living to move beyond death into the afterlife, while others are observed reenacting either the scenario of their ultimate demise, or some specific horror that they experienced in the flesh. They are thought to be doomed to relive the suffering that holds them earthbound for eternity – a hell all its own.

The truth of the matter is that these spirits are not spirits at all, but are merely the shadows of a Soul that once walked the earth, its image reflecting across the pools of time to be glimpsed in moments when the unwitting observer's mind gives in to its more subtle surroundings. It is an echo that carries on forever through the vacuum of time, which is heard by the living and thought to be the immediate and present vocalization.

This is not to say that the shadows of the souls that have passed out of this world are not real, for they are. This is not to say that they are to be ignored entirely, for although there is nothing we can do for them in their state of limbo, there is a good deal they can do for us. These gossamer echoes dwell in a region very near to earth, between the physical and the astral planes, but closer to here than there. This allows them to be seen and heard in quiet moments, and it also allows them to meddle in affairs, if they are so inclined.

Rarely will a spirit of the dead act upon this world of his own initiative, as it is just as illusive to him as his world is to us. Most poltergeist hauntings and threatening spectral visitations are of a demonic, rather than a necrotic nature. The dead are empty shells of a being that once was, having no purpose or directive, but simply existing like the visible star beam whose source had burnt out millennia ago. As such, any direction is not only welcomed, but also devoured. The weak and withered form of the spirit of the dead can be seen mutating in the moment that a command is give, sometimes becoming youthful and exuberant, other times becoming fierce.

The dead travel fast, when a destination is set. They do not have the innate power to instantly align the stars to the Necromancer's will, as do the angels, nor do they have the spiritual stamina to inflict disease bit by bit to cause the death of an enemy a decade after the command is given, but for minor miracles, the potency of the dead is never diminished.

It seems that in their tortured state, they too may spread torture. The spirits of the dead work fast and hard to bring misery to an enemy of the Operator, usually such suffering taking seat in the mind of the foe, beginning with nightmares, and in some cases ending with suicide. If the Operator can cause several of the deceased spirits to crowd around the mortal adversary, the end of that enemy is guaranteed to be swift.[3]

Wandering Spirits

When my interest and experience in the occult began moving beyond that of a Dabbler, I naturally began to align myself with those whose Ascendant nature carried them towards a similar path. It was a fun, although probably a socially abnormal activity for us to drive thirty or so miles out of the city into the middle of the southwest desert or sandstone and sagebrush hills at night. Even in the darkest hours, the red sand and rock held the warmth that the sun had given it in the day, and the giant moon spread its light across every bush and cactus and silhouetted the jagged mountains on the horizon.

We piled out of the cramped, compact cars that were volunteered to make the journey over sharp rock and soft sand for thirty minutes, and gathered in a circle, every person facing the center. After smoking our cigarettes and jostling each other with banter, the group went quiet, each congregant sensing the impending adventure gathering its critical mass. Cigarettes were extinguished and hands were joined, until the circle of friends was connected as one circuit. I would usually begin the oration as the organizer of the event, calling out into the warm night sky, "We join hands together as Brothers of Darkness, and we welcome the Powers of Darkness to enter this circle."

Our eyes would close and our breaths would align with one another's as we sensed the collective power of our gathering and that power sweeping into the circle from the outside. Our minds would focus and our energy would rise to give force to our commands.

"Any spirits that can hear our voices show yourselves! Enter this circle and join us as your Brothers. All spirits in this area come now."

Another congregant would add to the impromptu invocation, "Demons and spirits of the night hear our call and answer it. Rise up from the dust and greet us."

Others were free to give requests or commands for the Summoning of these entities, although most would simply open their awareness to that which we were calling forth. Either often we would see, in our minds or by our eyes countless spirit forms moving towards us, bounding through the desert towards the circle like rabid jackrabbits, clamoring to reach those that had dared to invite them in.

45

Once the nameless entities were present, we were usually at a loss for any exact command or desire aside from their simple manifestation. Knowing that we could not just call them up to say hello, one of us would offer some vague and half-hearted instruction, such as, "Every spirit that has answered our call, grant us power and strength."

An equally sincere call for departure was issued, the circle was broken, and we would return home... sometimes not alone.

The entities that we would call through these makeshift conjurations are what can be referred to as "wandering spirits." These entities at times may attempt to communicate with the Dabbling Magician through Ouija boards, although their power is so diminished as to disallow them from moving the planchette across the board with any great strength. They also do not possess the potency for poltergeist activity, or many other forms of materialization or effect on the physical plane. Wandering spirits are aimless, barely self-aware energy forms. In his book, Modern Magick, Donald Michael Kraig calls these spirits "astral nasties," and warns against allowing them to usurp the Magician's time and energy.[4] I must agree that aside from their entertainment value, there is little worth in dealing with these entities at all.

Aside from these most basic and most common entities which the Magician may evoke once the formulae and the practice is learned, there are others which may seem unconstrainable or even untouchable, the likes of which the Ascendant Sorcerer will also summon forth to visible appearance. In time, even the Gods may appear before the throne of the incarnate Master, and will fulfill his requests.

Chapter Three
Preparatory Works

The Dabbling Evocator will often attempt at least one evocation ritual before realizing that perhaps he has not prepared himself for such an advanced Operation. Reviewing the elementary principles of evocation outlined in the first chapter of this text, it is obvious to most – even those who have been performing evocations with some success – that there is work to be done in preparation for the materialization of the spirits.

Preparatory Immersion

In order to fulfill the demands of the first principle of evocation, the Aspirant must enter the Temple with absolute expectation of the ritual's success. While he may "talk himself up" or even deceive himself temporarily, the moment that the first words of the incantation are spoken, all bravado will melt. Careful study not only of the grimoire or text from which you will be evoking, but also of accounts of those who *have* had success with the specific entity that you will be evoking will prove to be a crucial step in solidifying your resolve to have nothing but a successful evocation. Although the best occult support and advice has historically been found in, and often restricted to various esoteric orders throughout the ages, the modern ritualist is fortunate in our time's unique advantage of a world connected through internet, relatively unregulated literature, magazines, various subcultural clubs, and thousands of other ways that individuals may converse with others one-on-one from across the globe. This racial connection both works *for* the Magician in that he has access to information and even accounts of personal experiences within the occult, yet it also works *against* him, in that the greater volume of information, the thinner the gold of it is spun.

As I was tinkering with my own methods of evocation in search of that one supreme ritual capable of thrusting Satan himself into my bedroom with a cloud of smoke and a burst of flame, I would keep the questions that I knew to be silly from the Masters that I studied under, and I would seek out Sorcerers only a step or two ahead of me, to leech as much advice and direction as possible. At that stage in my Magickal progression, I was using a scrying mirror through which I could communicate with the evoked entity, and asking for the advice of the various other struggling Practitioners in trying to perfect this method of communication, I would often get replies like, "You have to make sure that your mirror is at exactly a 45 degree angle," or "Make sure that the sigil is placed perfectly centered in the Triangle, because you know that if it's not, the demon won't show up." In hundreds of these tidbits of blind guesses, once in a while I would hear a sentence or two capable of changing my entire approach to Magick, such as, "Blow out the candles, forget about the mirror, and know that what you see before you is actually before you."

When searching for information about the entity that you're planning to evoke, it is best to turn to those who have evoked that very same entity more than once, and have resultantly reaped rewards. Avoid asking the questions of, "How do I?" because you already know. The information is already here, in these pages, and is often even already tucked in your hidden reptilian brainstem just waiting to be released by the right combination of words and will. Ask about the entity as if you're asking about a beautiful woman or an impressive man. Discover through your conversations the curves of her body or the depth of his gaze. Learn the spirit's temperament, the roughness, or gentleness of its voice, the candor of its replies. Learn to see the spirit, long before *your* evocation, as a real and tangible being.

An important part of your preparatory immersion is seemingly in exact opposition to the advice given above: do not speak of the evocation, or of the spirit outside of these conversations.

So many Neophytes in evocation want to share their new powers with the world, to let everyone know how truly important they are to be learning the ancient art of summoning spirits. I guarantee you, your power *will* change the world, and your importance will be made manifest. Moreover, if no one knows how important you are, your effect will be all the greater. The moment that you consider sharing your new knowledge with others, doubt enters your being. In actuality, the desire to talk with the uninitiated about these matters is a sign of your doubt and your need for reassurance. You will not find it in them, this is also assured. Your relationship with the demon, angel, spirit, or elemental that you have chosen is indeed a sacred one, a personal relationship. Study all of the information that you can about the entity. Question those who have held the same personal relationship with it. In addition, go about your life in the outside world with a sure knowledge that your experience is a unique one.

If these simple practices of identifying with the spirit, and then viewing the information that you gather as sacred and personal, much like a friend's secret that you have sworn to never reveal, are held to, days of candleburning rituals or Holy Communions preceding the ritual of evocation will never be necessary.

Invocation of Omnipotence

Indisputably, the best method by which the aspiring Evocator may discover his or her own sense of omnipotence is to act as God would act, not in holiness or piety, but in power. As the Sorcerer succeeds in ritual after ritual, whether his Magick is that of candles, elements, herbs, or incantations, the rationalizations of coincidence fade and leave him with the understanding that he has power - that indeed he *is* power incarnate. It is actually this power and the successes that the Dabbler begins to experience as he puts the Works of Magick into effect that drives most Aspirants back into the arms of orthodox religion or no religion at all. Magick is fun and exciting, until the spirits that are called appear and the universe les and obeys the command of the Invoker. For those who hold on to the flames rising in them and ride the whirlwind into Eternity, the realization of their literal Godhood is not far.

It is necessary, however, that the student gets a glimpse of his true, endless power, without being required to present a resume documenting years of hands-on experience of materializing solid manifestations of power and will. While there are many meditations, visualizations, and even complete rituals that have been constructed and exclusively used through the past few centuries of occult philosophy, I have found the following contemplation invokes a perfect balance between humility in the face of an ageless and limitless power, and confidence in wielding that power.

Before beginning, it is recommended that you find a place wherein you may conduct your Operations without being disturbed at any time of the day, and which is accessible enough to facilitate frequent visits without hardship. Initially, the Aspirant may think that his bedroom, living room, or other common area will suffice. It usually will not. The area that you choose, which is to become your Temple, should not be used for any other purpose than for the Operations of Magick and ritual. It should be free from any wall or ceiling hangings, and should preferably be without windows and only one door by which you may enter. All furniture should also be removed from the room. In summation, the room should be shut off from the rest of the world. Once it is consecrated, it will indeed become a vacuum in the spatial universe, untouched and untouchable.

Set a chair in the center of the room, facing north. Close your eyes and allow yourself thirty seconds to acclimate. Sit up in the chair, straightening your spine and opening your airways, and take a deep breath in. Remain conscious of the air entering your mouth, flowing down your throat, and flooding your lungs. Hold the breath for a moment, long enough to feel your lungs, chest, and your entire torso stretched in the expansion. Let the breath out and notice the relaxation of your entire body and even your mind. Take another breath and give the same attention to your body's reaction to it as you inhale, hold, and exhale. As you continue breathing in such a manner, these observations will begin to interest your mind; you will find yourself somewhat amused at the specific physiology that you have not paid great attention to in this past.

Once this stage of interest is reached, take your attention from your body and move it into your environment. With your eyes either opened or closed, view the room in which you sit. Rather than studying the walls and the floor, let your eyes focus on the air that surrounds you. Inhale deeply; hold the breath momentarily, and exhale, keeping your visual or imaginative attention on the air in the room. Take a few of these deep breaths and feel each one connecting you to your environment as you breathe it in and give your breath back to it.

Either visualize, once again with your eyes open or closed the particles of air around you. See them in your mind drifting through the air carelessly, wafting about the room without destination or purpose, but merely existing around you. Continue to breathe in a deep, controlled manner as you observe your invisible environment, but allow the breaths to simply come to you, facilitating your peace and security in the room. As you look on at the countless particles of air around you, see them slowly taking on light, as if they are absorbing the little bit of sun or artificial light that has crept into the room, and reflecting that light all around them like microscopic prisms. At this point, it is best to continue the visualization with your eyes open. If you are not able at first to see these things with your physical sight, simply allow your awareness of it to pervade your mind as you look around the room. Know that this is happening and sense it, even if your eyes and your logical mind try to sway you.

As you view the tiny particles of light, as you become aware of them as more than molecules of air, see that they begin to glow brighter, the light spreading farther from their centers, shining like a million suns surrounding you. Relax your brow, relax your eyes, relax your mind, and allow this image to become clear to you – so clear that although your senses cannot perceive it, your mind does not doubt it. Soon, the air around you should seem as if it is aglow from wall to wall, the warm light filling the entire room. Again, whether your senses can perceive this or not, know that it is a real occurrence rather than an imaginary construct. Know that you are no longer visualizing, but that you now perceive.

Open your inner senses to the light that fills the room, rather than observing it through your superficial mental abilities. Feel the warmth of it. Feel the glow touching you and pulsing through the air. Connect with the buzzing light around you in an emotional or intuitive way, feeling its presence and discerning the purity of it. Close your eyes, and as darkness covers your vision, feel the particles of shining light still beaming around you. Penetrate the light with your intuition, sensing that it is the Light of creation, of healing, of life. Probe deeper into the core of each particle of light

51

with your senses, and feel the power radiating from within. Sense the awesome dynamic force that the light carries with it, the ability to expand and create unknown universes, or to superheat and incinerate those galaxies that have existed for billions of years. Allow these sensations to run through you. Rather than simply resting in your brain, let the magnitude of it fill you, until you can look out at the invisible particles of light with a familiarity and awe.

Inhale, and as you do so feel the currents of air that are sweeping towards your mouth also carrying these omnipresent particles of light towards you, as the air has become the light. It is essential that you not give in to the force of the swoon that may come over you at this point. You must not allow yourself to drift into a sleep-like state, or to "zone out." Doing so is your brain's automatic reaction to something that is beyond the flesh. Breathe the light in, and experience it. Feel the warmth and the power of the light entering your mouth and your throat. Rather than moving to your lungs, sense and visualize it filling your torso, tingling your insides, glowing within you. As you breathe out, instead of releasing the Magickal, purifying light, instead release your worry, apprehension, fear, guilt from past mistakes, or any other negating energies that have stored themselves inside of you. You can visualize this negative energy as a brown oily mist that seeps from your mouth as you exhale. The pure light that still fills the room cannot be soiled, but rather dissipates the noxious energy the instant that it leaves your mouth. Repeat the inhalation of spiritual light, allowing with each breath the healing properties of it to effect you, feeling it restoring your tissues and organs to prime health, cleaning the blood that flows through your body, and purging the webs from your heart. Like the virtue that passed from Jesus to the hemorrhaging woman when she touched the hem of his garments and was instantly healed[1], feel this healing force entering you with every particle of air, yet with as much as you take into yourself, the light in the room is not diminished, but is an overflowing well of power and light.

When you feel that you are full of light and can take in no more, close your eyes and turn your attention entirely inwards. Feel the light that is now inside of yourself, glowing like a thousand suns. Feel it radiating, bursting out through your skin, not content to be trapped in a prison of flesh but free to create. Notice the tingling of your skin as this pure, creative light spreads out from you. Visualize it as an ever-expanding aura of fiery brilliance emanating from you, the center of light. The physical sensation will be more pronounced in your face, your arms, and your hands. Let the light travel out from you from these areas, as well as from everywhere in you.

Turn your attention to the center of your chest, and feel the light pushing its way out from that area, beaming from your heart like an endless fountain of love. Let your hands fall to your sides with your palms up and let your fingers curve inwards naturally. Sense the light and power spreading out from your hands, waiting if forever to be directed to some goal.

Once the sensation of the light emanating from you is no longer imagined, but is a solid current running through your being, take a long, deep breath in. As you hold the breath for a moment, bring to your mind an appreciation for the greatness of the power that is within you. Know that it is the same force and intelligence that fashioned the universes, this power that you have brought into yourself. Breathe out and release your tension. Inhale once more, long and deep, and again reflect on the magnitude of the light within. Identify the power of this light with the power that you hold. Know that with this light and power within you, if you make any command with the fullness of your will and without reservation or fear, all of existence would stir and would rumble to answer you. Do not allow the innate sense of overwhelming grace and humility to hold you captive, as is possibly the strongest anti-urge that is produced with any form of invoking omnipotence. Instead, take these emotions that would otherwise lend towards weakness and let them flow from you, out of your hands, eyes, and mouth, spreading the light within into the darkness of the lower worlds, bringing all things under the power of your will.

Once the power and the light has been consciously made a part of the Self, you will likely feel an urging to do something with it, to act in some way, as simple as a trickled tear and a whispered "thank you," as dramatic as the dances and gyrations of a Pentecostal, or as terrifying as using that invisible yet very tangible force to Summon into physical being an entity that is timeless and powerful without end. Again, this is another urge that at this point must be resisted. If the omnipotence which flows through you, whether it is a slight "buzz" of Divine Current or an internal explosion of dynamic force, cannot be spent on trivial things, but must fuel the generator that will eventually give light to the stars. Close your eyes let your head fall back onto your shoulders so that you would see the ceiling or the sky above you, and let your mouth fall open. Relax all of your body, take in a deep breath, and hold it. Feel the light within you gathering in your chest, and as you exhale, feel it rushing out of your body into the air. Regain your previous posture, inhale slow and deep, hold the breath, feel the energy collecting in your chest, let your body go limp, your head tilt back, your mouth open, and release the breath until there is no more air in your lungs. Two or three repetitions of this discharge should clear you of the light that you have pulled into yourself, and will most often cause an extreme exhaustion. You will feel the tired glow that only arrives after intense intercourse, feeling like a numbing opiate swarming your soul and forcing your active mind into a dead slumber.

Repeat this exercise at least a few times, once daily, before each evocation that you perform, and feel the potency of it quickening with each repetition, allowing you to become comfortable in the presence of your own godhood, pushing your power to its critical mass, and invoking a portion of supreme omnipotence each time.

Ritual Tools

Modern Hermetic Magicians, specifically the adherents of systems derived from the Hermetic Order of the Golden Dawn, are notorious for their arsenal of ritual tools and implements. They carefully select or fashion their ritual garments and robes after either ancient Egyptian or Hebrew ceremonial dress, often stitching emblems or lines of numerological value into the cloth, and they complete the costume with an ornate headdress that would make most Practitioners not of that discipline so uncomfortable and self conscious as to spoil the whole of the ritual with distraction. Upon their altars, which are two square boxes of equal dimensions fastened to one another in an attempt to symbolize the union of the microcosm and the macrocosm, they place a wooden tablet that is painted with the Enochian elemental words in colors concordant with each element. In addition to this "Tablet of Union," a tablet is also placed on each of the four walls in the Temple, each one painted in the solid color of the element relating to that cardinal direction and inscribed with that element in the Enochian language. Aside from the basic ritual wand and dagger, the Magician is to procure a double-edged dagger that he will paint yellow. When the paint dries, he is to write in the Hebrew language in purple paint or ink the names, "Shaddai El Chai, Raphael, Chassan, Ariel, Hiddikel Mizrach," and "Rauch." The sigils of each of these entities are also to be drawn on the handle of the Air Dagger. A Fire Wand is to be constructed using an 8-inch wooden dowel with a magnetized wire running through the center of it with a decorative wooden "acorn" cap on the top of it. After priming the wand, yellow acrylic paint is to be applied to the head of the wand, as well as four ¾-inch bands equally spaced down the rod of the wand. Once that paint has dried, the Magician must carefully paint the remainder of the wand red. On this, he is to inscribe the names, "YHVH TZABAOTH, Michael, Aral, Seraph, Pison, Darom," and "Aesch." A bowl or cup is used for the element of water, and a pentacle is used for the elemental earth, both being equally as ornate and inscribed as the Air Dagger and Fire Wand.[2] These "basic" ritual tools are just the beginning; some Magicians engraving rings of various metals with pentacles and sigils that might bring the spirits under his control, draping the Temple in silk of colors favored by the Summoned, Protective Circles drawn like murals on the floor, headbands with gems that might amplify the faculties of the Third Eye, sandals or other clothing items actually fashioned from the hair of a camel, etc.

All of this seems rather compensatory, and is merely a very long route to the fulfillment of the third principle of evocation: attainment of omnipotence. While most modern ritualists use the Hermetic system of evocation in the "spirit of tradition," and the inherent beauty of the system rather than as an expedient means to an end, for all practical purposes, the extravagant ritual tools in themselves have no virtue.

It can rightly be argued that the Hermetic system is one whose aim is spiritual attainment rather than lucre, and in that vein the whole of the system and all of the trinkets involved are essential to the entire effect of the thing. The procuring, construction, decoration, and consecration of these tools in the manner described above, or in any other manner that some might find ridiculously superfluous, does however meet the necessary requirements of the second principle of evocation, which is the reliable use of a working system. Concomitantly, the fact stands that these very Works are in themselves acts of Ascent, each evocation teaching the Summoner more about his own powers, abilities, knowledge, and Godhood, and the rewards reaped are only reaffirmations of this self-understanding that is achieved. As such, if the Aspirant desires to evoke using the system of the Golden Dawn, he may very well do so, and with no less success than the original system that is presented in this text. If the flashing colors and the flashy words impede the immediate progress of the Evocator, however, the few implements listed and described below will not only suffice, but will be those simple and unimpressive tools which carve the universe from the flesh of the gods that they have slain.

1. A ritual dagger is needed for these Operations, symbolic of the Will of the Evocator. The handle of the dagger must be black, and the length of the blade must be at least six inches. Despite the advice of the neo-pagan white light mentors who would have ye harm none in any similitude, if the blade is not sharp upon purchase it should be made so. It is also appearing to be the trend to seek out on the walls of the occult shops and pawnbrokers the most ornate, jeweled, gothic-looking daggers to use in ritual. Avoid these pretty distractions, and attempt to keep the dagger as nondescript as possible.

2. A brass, tin, or silver chalice should be obtained, being made entirely of the chosen metal rather than a veneer or plate. The cup should also bear no specific markings or engravings. Despite the obvious relation to the element of water and all that such a correlation may symbolize to those that look for such signs, the chalice has the ritual purpose of holding liquid. The type of metal and the design of the cup only have virtue in the ability to contain the energies that will imbue the said liquid as it is used in ritual.

3. An altar is also needed for the rituals of Evocation. Although various types of altars exist and may be used for diverse ritual Workings, the Operations of evocation are best facilitated best by a table-like altar. A small bedside table will work, although the height of the altar needs to allow you to comfortably rest your hands on the top of it

during ritual, as well as read from books or notes that are placed thereon. Ideally, the altar should be made level with your waistline. For this reason, either building one or modifying a nightstand to reach this height is usually much easier than searching for one to buy. A simple box made of particleboard or composite wood can be constructed, creating a rectangle of the afore-mentioned subjective height with a base and top of about 2 feet squared. Either a natural wood color or a solid matte black should be used in order to keep the mind from the altar and upon the Working at hand.

These three ritual tools are all that is needed to successfully perform evocation to physical materialization. While the Evocator may choose to use the beautiful and elaborate systems of the Kabbala, the silk and gems of Gardnerian forms, or the black robes and thick staffs of Traditional Satanism, such is a choice, and the choice may also be made, with no less success, to discard the pretty things and to Ascent just as well.

Ritual Mandalas and Circles

Central to the performance of any ritual, be it demonic or deific in nature, being performed by teenage Dabblers, Master Evocators, or Christian clergy, is the Circle. Often in religious ceremony which takes on a more superficial tone rather than a deeply esoteric one, such as the Mass and Eucharist of the Catholics, the Sacraments and Temple Ordinances of the Mormons, or the marriage and funeral rites of all, the Circle is sent to the background of the Operation: the circle of the chalice of Christ's blood and the round wafer of His flesh; the floors and ceiling of traditional churches are usually decorated with circular images, sometimes being as ornate as a large circles made in goldleaf or stonework; or the arrangement or construction of the ceremonial area itself is one large circle.

Throughout all religion, the circle has come to represent infinity, the eternal nature of all things, as well as the connection between all things. This has taken the form in ancient mythology as the image of Ouroboros, the tail-eating serpent that has appeared by different names in nearly every culture, despite geographical isolation from one another. The circle is the supreme symbol for completion, for the powers of heaven descending to earth and the mortal offerings ascending to heaven. In alchemy, it is the continuation of the cycle of everything from mercury to salt to sulfur and back to mercury. In the philosophy of the transmigration of the soul, the Wheel of Eighty-Four, or the wheel of birth, death, and reincarnation, is the great circle for which the whole of the universe is sustained.

The initial assumption by the Neophyte or the outsider is that the Circle, when used in rites of evocation, is constructed and consecrated for the purpose of protecting the Evocator from those being and forces which he dares to call forth. Being witness to the ease in which the demons rend the life of an enemy at his command, or destroy that life altogether, or by which the angels lift a man from poverty and illness, or even from the threshold of death, and deliver him into the throne room of the Kings, the Adept knows better than to believe that he is protected from the godlike powers of his astral emissaries by a circle. He knows that even *if* the Circle is fortified with all of the spiritual armament available, he cannot remain within it forever, and the spirits that he has called are everywhere, swarming the skies, and flowing through the mountains.

The Circle as it is used in evocation represents the origin point of all things, the initial Eternal center from which existence itself first flowed. It is from this point, in the center of the Circle in which the Evocator stands, that all that he seeks to manifest will be brought forth. It is not, as is often explained in modern occult philosophy, representative of the whole of the universe encapsulated into one unique space, but is instead the centrifuge of creation.

The Circle can also be seen as simply the place that has been set aside for the Evocator to stand and Operate. Likewise, a place is set aside for the Summoned, and that place is the Triangle of Manifestation. Although in the more advanced Operations of evocation that are given in this book the Triangle is not always employed, it is necessary for the majority of evocations that you will perform for any specific task, which will be the simple calling forth of one entity for one purpose. The myth has arisen over time that the act of evocation lures the entity into materialization within the Triangle, tricking and trapping it within a spiritual prison that it cannot escape until it has sworn its allegiance and service to the Evocator. The perpetuators of this myth know little about the nature of the entities that they claim to evoke, and even less about their own position in existence. The entities that are evoked, whether they are demonic, angelic, elemental, planetary, Qlippothic or Sephirotic, are obliged to fulfill the desires of the Magician so long as those desires are in alignment with the nature of the specific entity. The spirit enters the Triangle when it is used because that is the place that has been set aside for it to enter. It is the base of that spirit's materialization, the platform on which it may enter this world in a solid form.

Ritual purists insist that the Circle and Triangle need to be constructed in a permanent way, either drawn on the Temple floor never to be erased, made of wood or cloth to be laid out before the evocation, or in some way made to be used each and every time that the Summoning is performed. While this may be done, and most likely will be easier for the Operator than to remake them each time in a unique way, there are definite advantages in taking the time before each Operation to do so.

In many Eastern traditions, as well as in Native American spirituality, decorative mandalas have been used to sanctify an area, to call very specific forces into that area, and to effect the immediate environment and inhabitants in a particular way. Although for the purposes of evocation, mandalas like those found in Hinduism or Buddhism are a bit too extensive and involved to be practical; the basic principle provides a wealth of possibilities for the Evocator to utilize in further empowering his rituals and for a more solid materialization of the entities that he evokes.

Each mandala used in evocation should be unique to that entity, its sphere of origin, or to the goal for which the Operation is being performed. It should also be drawn or constructed no sooner than one hour and no longer than twelve hours preceding the actual evocation ritual. Modern Practitioners seem to have lost their patience with everything, especially the Works that will open the doors to Eternity. They have no time to wait and prepare for a state which supersedes time itself, so one minute before they intend to evoke, they move their altar, dagger, and chalice into the center of a room, toss the grimoire on the altar along with some sheets of notebook paper, quickly scribble the sigil of the entity, and trace an imaginary Circle on the ground with their fingers. The proverb,

"You reap what you sow," is never more applicable than with the delicate Works of Magick. Taking the time to retreat to the Temple, to carefully draw the mandala on the floor, to set the altar in the true center of that Circle, to set the candles, tools, and resources upon it, and then to wait until the hour and minute is at hand to evoke will prove to be an irreplaceable process that will not only allow the full materialization of the entity, but also allows the complete manifestation of your will.

The mandala that you use for any evocation does not need to be ornate and detailed at all. A simple Circle drawn on the ground with a three-foot diameter will work; a similar Circle with the names of the ruling angels of the Sephirotic or Qlippothic rulers of the original sphere of the entity written on the border, or of Divine or Diabolic Names relating to the entity, or the entities name itself will be even better. In some more obscure traditions the name of the Summoned can be broken into four letters or syllables with each one written on the border of the Circle in the position of each cardinal direction; the same may be done with the sigil of the entity.

Fashioning a mandala from the natural elements is a potent way in which a Circle can be made unique to the spirit or the goal. A ring of fire made on the ground with some slow-burning material is a nearly unmatched mandala for the evocation of demons, or for Baneful Works. Pouring regular petroleum over Styrofoam until you are left with a thick, sticky syrup is an excellent fuel for this type of fiery mandala. Similarly, for Operations of peace, love, intellectual pursuits, health, and harmony, a small mote can be dug about six inches deep in the form of the Circle and filled with water. If the evocation is aimed at improving prosperity and finances, for building physical strength or endurance, for having influence in social, political, religious, or business matters, or for any other concrete desire, a simple ring of stones may be placed in a Circle around the altar and Working space of the Evocator. The same materials can be used to form the Triangle in which the entity will manifest.

Once you have decided what you would like to achieve in your life through evocation, have decided on what spirit is best suited for that task, you should then decide what type of mandala would create the best environment for the materialization of the spirit and the origin for the eventual accomplishment of your goal.

If the Evocator should feel the need to confess his sins to a minister ordained by some particular church, to commune with the spirit to be summoned in a more subtle manner, or to invoke the essence of the planetary sphere of the entity before performing the ritual of evocation, he may certainly do so. In such, however, he is appeasing only himself, and often his superstitions that will in time work against him. The basic principles of evocation fulfill their own prophesies in the same manner that once you jump from a cliff, gravity will indeed pull you towards the earth or the sea below, whether you believe it will or not. Most Practitioners pay homage to venerated superstitions because they instinctively know this, and they are afraid to jump for fear of the natural governing laws fulfilling the duties of their placement in the universe. Once the twin giants of fear and doubt are slain, evocation is seen to be a remarkably simple tool to use. Moreover, once that discovery is made, it becomes clear that it is not a tool of man, but it is the tool of the Gods, and its power without fail will unlock and open the doors to their palace.

Chapter Four
The Vision and the Voice

The one point in which the ritual of evocation is thought to have failed in when the spirit begins to materialize, and the Neophyte is unable to communicate with it in any significant manner. He prepares himself psychologically for the evocation, learns to accept the flow of omnipotence through him, prepares a ritual Temple in which the spirit may manifest, and he gives the incantation with the necessary potency. Then he waits patiently. His patience quickly wears and gives way to doubt, and when the spirit still fails to materialize before him, his heart sinks, he closes the ritual, and he drags his feet back to his home.

A division has been occurring between two very distinct occult philosophies in regard to the materialization of spirits, and it is a division that has been long needed. On one hand, there are those who have spent years developing their ability to see, hear, smell, and feel those things that hide just beyond the normal range of sensation, usually through the disciplines of scrying, remote viewing, or sensory attunement. As the Sorcerer begins to recite the incantations and conjurations, he opens his scrying vision and connects his awareness to that of the spirit. The conjurations then call that spirit into the Temple, at which point the Evocator guides it into the Triangle of Manifestation, wherein it will construct a body from the smoke of the incense or the vapors of cooling sacrificial blood. His senses will fully awaken and fix upon the materializing apparition until he is able to view it as concretely as any construct of the physical plane.

On the other hand, there is the school of thought which insists that the endeavors on the part of the Operator to train his finer senses to observe and record the occurrences of the spiritual entities and currents are in vain, and it is only when the ritual is performed correctly, without flaw or deviation, as is put forth in the grimoire specific to the spirit (and often in accordance with the supposed spiritual laws presented by Orthodox religion), the Summmoned will automatically manifest before the Magician. If the heart, spirit, and mind of Evocator is pure, and if the Holy Spirit rushes into him, his incantations, and conjurations will bring the entity into full materialization independent of his own prior ability to behold such things. Again, this understanding of the nature of materialization is based a good deal on the teachings of Orthodox religion, specifically Catholicism, and these fundamentalists rarely demonstrate acceptance for or patience with any system or discipline, which does not pay homage to that original Church but, instead involves itself in forms of idolatry and paganism. When the Magician recites his incantations and conjurations, usually taking a more threatening and condemning tone than the former, the spirit will still appear, he will still hold intercourse with the Summoned, and will still receive benefit there.

If the Evocator has properly induced the necessary preparatory immersion, and is standing in the ritual Circle with omnipotence flowing through him, he will indeed auto-matically sense the Summoned entering the Temple. If the elementary principles of evocation are held to, the spirit will enter, and will manifest. Moreover, if the Operator has disciplined himself to consciously examine and interpret the form and figure of that manifestation, he will indeed see it. If he has not, then he relies entirely on a state of spiritual fugue, where his meaty brain is so overwhelmed and his physical senses are so assaulted that visions begin to dance around him and the spirit will materialize within the Triangle.

An interesting difference between the two is in the materialization itself. The latter type of Evocator, he who does not prepare himself psychically for the viewing of the spirit, will often experience intense phenomenon preceding the actual materialization of the spirit he has called. As endorphins, dopamine, and neuropeptids flood the brain, lights will flash and dance around him, fog or smoke will fill the room, voices will shout out from the darkness or thumps and pounds will be heard on the walls; often armies of spirits will fill the room and sing in choirs, or black slithering shapes will threaten the sanctity of the Circle. The phenomenon will reach a devastating height, the psychological and sensory impact of the whole thing disturbing the Magician's equilibrium and will cause him to begin to swoon, and then the Summoned will appear. In direct contrast, the former Evocator, he who spends years perfecting his spiritual senses, will sense the energies building in the Temple, will feel them growing stronger and gathering a definite mass, and will guide them through his will towards the Triangle, wherein the energies will coagulate and will mingle with the incense smoke to form a materialized being with which he may converse. This same contrast is seen in the results achieved by either side. Usually, when the Evocator retains control over his senses throughout, he will command the entity to bring to pass a very specific thing. That thing, and no other, will manifest itself in his life in the next few days. The one variance that can be considered major is that he may receive slightly more or slightly less than requested, or it will reach him in a manner not foreseen. Nevertheless, he achieves to near exactness that which he intended through the ritual. When the Evocator who relies solely on the grace of God and on the Divinity of the Operation itself is presented with the moment of making his demands, he will usually battle the Summoned with words and wit, and a psychic battle will ensue until one or the other has been subjugated. If the Magician is the victor, he will make his demands and will dismiss the spirit to carry them. The next few days or weeks are usually rather tumultuous. He will have money come to him rather spontaneously, and then be taken away again. He will on one day be the friend and confidant of everyone, and the next he will seem the scourge of the earth. He will experience great love and great loss. And somewhere in that mix, he will be able to say, "I got what I asked for."

The automatic and the autonomic collide in reality. When the principles of evocation, which are universal, are kept to, the spirits will draw near and will manifest within the Temple. Most occult Practitioners, however, approach ritual with a more scientific expectation rather than a religious one, and it is rare to find such an occultist that is prone to the fervor of the Pentecostal or the fearful faith of the Catholic to the extent necessary to induce the chemical reactions in the brain which would cause hallucinations to coincide with the astral occurrences produced by the ritual. While the phenomenon, which is easily argued as a self-induced state of temporary psychosis or even schizophrenia, and the hallucinations which follow are nearly unmatched, the whole Operation leaves the hands of the Operator and puts him at the whim of the visions and noises that impales him and the dizzying "Holy Spirit" that will not allow him pride or ego.

When the conjuration is spoken, calling the spirit to appear, the room will fill with a quick thickening force, and that force will be known to be intelligent and ancient, despite the previous training of the Evocator. Through his will alone, the Magician guides the buzzing and popping energy into the Triangle, which will allow it to condense and to form actual particles of matter, albeit a finer matter than flesh and bone. It is at this point that the Sorcerer will need to ready himself to communicate with the spirit by the means that he has chosen.

As the scientific and verifiable aspects of evocation first began to fall under the microscopes of the philosophers of the middle part of the previous millennium, very few who believed that they had the power or the Divine Decree to summon forth the spirits felt that they were also blessed with the ability to see and hear the spirits that they constrained. It was common practice, then, to bring into the ritual Temple a practiced clairvoyant or a natural empath who would be able to translate the raw, spiritual intercourse into meaningful conversation, and thereby act as a translator or conveyor between the Summoner and the Summoned. While commanding spirits was formerly known to be not only the privilege but also the obligation of a man of God, to speak with them directly was the practice of a witch or heretic. As our faith and fear in God has waned, our belief and confidence in ourselves has grown. There is not a person reading this text who, given the appropriate instruction and the diligent work necessary, would ever need another person to do for them that which they can do for themselves.

An astounding number of people that I have met as I have learned and taught firsthand the secrets of evocation have reported that while they can summon forth a spirit with relative ease, and can sense that spirit in the room with them, they cannot, no matter how hard they try, see the spirit, hear its voice, or in any way communicate with it. One gentleman who had been practicing evocation for nearly 20 years would use a pendulum to pick up the intent of the demons that he would evoke. Showing me this method in an actual evocation, he drew a small circle on a piece of paper and divided it into perfect quarters by means of two intersecting diametric lines. At the top of the circle he wrote "yes," on the bottom he wrote "no" - to the left was also "no," and to the right was "yes." As I saw him do this, my mind returned to my teenage ouija board sessions, and I could not help but to roll my eyes and sigh. We both sat in meditation for a moment, and then simultaneously invoked the omnipotent force that was required to perform the Operation. He drew the sigil of the demon that he intended to summon, and I continued my silent meditation as he charged the seal with the will of the evocation. In unison, we looked at one another in recognition of the appearance of the demon. We could feel it enter the room like a creeping fog, and gather around the Circle waiting to be directed. Combining our powers of will, we directed the accumulating force into the Triangle, and fed that power with our will until it had condensed into a body as solid as it could – one which I could see and one which he could not deny was there. He held the pendulum a few inches from the surface of his paper guide and greeted the demon.

"Demon N., are you present?" he asked, as was his customary initial question. The pendulum didn't move. My friend smiled and replied, "Thank you for attending us, and welcome to our Temple. We have Summoned you here…" and he continued with the exact desires for which we were performing the ritual. "Are you able to do complete these tasks without incident?" The pendulum didn't move. My friend replied, "Thank you. Do you then agree to complete these tasks on our behalf?" The pendulum didn't move, and my friend concluded, "Demon N., we thank you for your speedy answer to our call, and for your powerful assistance. Go now and complete these tasks, and return again swiftly if you are called." He officially dismissed the demon and performed a post-ritual banishing to cleanse the area.

The moment that he finished recording the ritual in his journal, I turned to him in amazement. "The pendulum didn't move, not once!" I shouted. I didn't doubt the impressions that he had received from the Working, as my sight and my hearing had verified the responses that he too understood to be correct. What confounded me was his use of the pendulum at all. Standing by his side as I stared at the demon before us and as he looked intently at his pendulum and paper, I wondered if my friend was well.

"It's called nonphysical manifestation," he answered. "Just because it doesn't happen on the physical plane doesn't mean it doesn't happen. The pendulum didn't physically move, but if it had, it would have moved upwards, towards the 'yes.'"

"How can you say that for sure?"

"Because," he said with a grin, "I could feel the pendulum tugging upwards, as if the magnetism in the entire room shifted for that one move. I could just feel it so strongly that I didn't need to see it."

Out of respect for my friend, I smiled and suggested we go to dinner.

It made more sense to me, after having witnessed his method of communication myself, and having verified the results of such with the face-to-face method that I had been using for most of my occult career, that he should leave the pendulum in the drawer, and rely on the *real* faculty which had allowed him to communicate. He seemed to me like a man who walked on a crutch although his broken leg had healed years ago. If my friend could so easily rely on his inner senses, which by his own admittance were in no way responsive to physical stimuli, why could he not do the exact same without the pendulum at all? People tend to search for signs and prophesies of good or ill fortune in cards, smoke, rippling water, weather patterns, and even the distant stars, all of which have no verifiable physical or chemical significance. Yet, they invariably refuse to trust the most instinctive senses that would allow them access to the most hidden secrets of power.

The greatest key in communicating with spirits is to calm your heart, relax your mind, reach out into your environment with you feelings, and then to trust them. While this alone will not allow you to "see" the spirit that stands before you, it does open up a pathway for conscious connection with that entity, and through that pathway the Vision will flow.

Nearly everyone, especially those who are drawn to the occult, has had the experience of feeling as though they are in the presence of a person who is deceased, or of some protective or formidable embodiment which they cannot see, hear, or smell, yet seems nonetheless real in that moment of contact. Unless the unseen visitor carries the aura of a loved one that is instantly recognizable, the observer rarely will attempt to put a face to the figure. They recognize its presence, categorize it according to their belief system, and deal with it in whatever manner that system – and their own immediate emotional response dictates. If, in that moment, the observer were to shut out all mental and emotional chatter, release expectation, and simply allow the senses to translate the spiritual image standing in the room with them, the likelihood of obtaining a very close, if not exact mental impression of the being would be great. We cannot sit and wait for a relative to pass away or for a ghost to come haunting, however, and it is more than foolish to perform a full evocation simply to see if you can pick up any impressions as to the appearance of the apparition. We can use a replicatible process by which a wandering spirit may be brought near to be observed. Notice that the said spirit is brought *near*, not brought *forth*. The difference between the two is immeasurable.

In order to experience firsthand contact with a spiritual entity or entities, you will need to set up a semi-proper Temple. Set your altar in the room that you have been using for your meditations thus far, facing west, upon which two white candles should be placed, both less than an inch from the north and south edges of the altar. Although the majority of evocation rituals will be performed standing, you will likely find it more comfortable to place a chair before the altar, so that when seated you will be looked towards the west and gazing between the candles. For this simple Operation, your dagger and chalice can be kept away.

Shut out all light from the Temple, light the candles on the altar, and seat yourself behind it. Close your eyes and enact the meditation that will invoke omnipotence. When your entire being is aglow with Divine Power and Light, and that force flows from your eyes, hands, and radiates from every pore in your skin, open your eyes, and let your gaze drift to the empty space between the white candles. Without looking directly into their flames, allow your peripheral vision to notice the light shining from the wicks, the aura that it creates, and the meeting of their orbs of light in that space on which your eyes are focused.

Take a deep breath in, retaining focus on that empty air above the altar, and feel the Godforce within you stirring as you breathe. Feel it gathering in your throat and in your mouth, ready to spill from your lips like a bursting dam of energy. Know that if the omnipotence is released from you in the form of words, all of existence and its countless inhabitants will be compelled to answer and to obey. Let the breath out by calling in a clear, controlled voice, "Spirits, hear my voice. Spirits, hear my call. Spirits, gather around me. Make yourselves known to me. I call you out of the shadows and out of the graves, and I command you to stand before me. Spirits, I compel you… come!"

Do not allow fear to plant even a single seed within you. Steady your heart, as it surely begins to thump as the wandering spirits' eyes move to your direction. Hold fast in a tranquil state, still aware of your own omnipotence as you sit and wait. As the conjuration was recited, if it was truly done so with Authority, you will have sensed the spirits bounding over the hills take notice of you. These spirits are by far the most willing to fly to your side and to make themselves known, and although for purposes of attainment or Ascent they are impotent, they are each unique and individual entities that you can observe.

Relax your gaze and let your vision blur slightly, taking the strain of observation off of your eyes and shifting it to your Other senses, which will begin to See from your Third Eye, in the center of your forehead. As you initially visualize the entities and receive impressions of their images, you will likely notice a fine pressure in the center of your forehead. When you encounter this, allow the energy that is trying to push its way from you, the invisible indigo ray of light that is attempting to burst into the Temple with its omniscience, to do so without restraint. Give your will over to your Greater powers, and trust in them when the time comes.

The first step in actually viewing the spirits present, even if only in your mental vision just yet, is to locate them. After you feel that the spirits that you have called near are indeed near, inhale, and hold the breath in your chest for a moment. Shut off your mind. It is vital that you not allow your brain to interfere with your comprehension by inserting its own images or critiquing those impressions that do surface. Slowly let the breath out. As you do so, sense your own intellectual awareness, your natural omniscience, flood the room. Sense the general location of the spirits, or if there are many, sense the location of the most powerful or the nearest one. Don't think, don't analyze, don't imagine; just receive. Your impressions at this point are not to originate in your mind, but are merely received by your mind. Feel the spirit's location in the same way that you can feel a stranger enter the room behind you. Remember, you are not performing an exercise in imagination, but are simply tuning your extant senses into a phenomenon that you have likely experienced in the past: the awareness of the presence of a non-physical entity.

Once the actual location of a spirit is discovered, train your senses on that space. Do not look at the space occupied by the spirit, keeping your gaze locked in the glow of the two white candles in the center of the altar. Simply stretch your senses and your awareness out to that one spot in the room. As you do this, your own conscious recognition of the presence of that particular spirit will grow stronger, sometimes frighteningly so. Bring your emotions back under your command, not reacting to your surroundings, but acting upon existence.

People learn about things through analyzing them, and they analyze things by asking themselves questions about them. Without questions, there can be no answers. Ask yourself, "How tall is this spirit?" Immediately, your mind will give you a response. If you have to search for an answer, it will not be true. Trust your senses, trust your answers, and trust yourself. Often, the moment the answer comes, with your eyes still gazing into the eternal glow of the candles' flames, you may see an outline of a figure through your peripheral vision in the spot where the spirit is known to stand. Do not focus on this, but continue focusing on that empty space before you.

Ask yourself now, "How is the spirit holding its body?" With this question, your mind will not longer attempt to answer in words, but will choose the easiest path by placing an image in your mind, or sometimes in that elusive peripheral vision. It is also at this point that the energies, those emanating from the multitude of spirits that have presented themselves, from the power of the ritual itself, and from your own God-State, will begin to overwhelm you, in collusion with your brain's inability to accept the impossible. This will cause a dizziness or lightheadedness, and it is often reported as a feeling of sinking through the floor, or general spatial imbalance. Remember to breathe and to gather yourself, and although the disorientation will not subside altogether, you will still be able to continue. You may as well be tempted strongly to let your eyes drift shut. Resist this, as it is a ploy to cease the barrage of spiritual reality on the illusion-soaked brain. Keep your eyes focused forward and allow the image of the stance of the spirit impress itself on your mind, or even on your vision.

As you see these things, it is vital not to relegate their value to the mind and imagination, but to place the importance of it on the reality of the spirit that stands in that disclosed location. As you see it in your mind, also sense it in your chest, in your heart, in that place within you that *knows* that you are in the presence of a thing that is beyond the flesh. As the impressions are transferred to your mind from the spirit, it is your duty in order to obtain a real image of it to then transfer the image back to that place where the spirit stands, rather than letting it dwindle in the unreal annals of the brain. Staring at the candle's glow, as the impression of the stance of the spirit comes to you, project this image back into its place of origin, seeing it either in your mind or your peripheral sight as standing in that stance before you. Hold this image in your mind maintaining it for a matter of at least a few seconds, sure that it is not going to vanish the moment that you take your attention away.

Ask yourself, "How does the spirit move?" What you are doing is step-by-step receiving and interpreting the whole figure of the spirit. You are lifting the veil between your mind and the spirit. When you ask this question, you will likely see the spirit begin to move. It is not that in asking this you cause the spirit to move, but rather that the spirit has been in motion as any living thing is, and in asking the question you are allowing your mind to observe this motion. The spirit therefore is not put into motion by your question, but it is your mind that is put into motion. You will see this outlined figure, which stands in a certain place at a certain height, and in a specific stance move its arms, hands, head, legs, or even mouth.

It is difficult to get this far in your uncovering of the image of the spirit without having perceived some of its more detailed features. Ask yourself slowly, "What is the appearance of the spirit's face?" For some reason that has eluded both myself and my spiritual associates, this question elicits the most dramatic response from the observer, often being the observation that ends the session of viewing for the moment. Sometimes the image of its face will flash in the mind immediately, and appears threatening or hideous, making it nearly impossible to retain conscious control over the emotions. Other times it may look pleasant, but as the mind attempts to analyze the details of it, the brain begins to shut down the whole of the process, always the enemy of Magick. The key to successfully working through this step is to avoid the details and to accept the general image. The body of the spirit is made of a finer matter than that of the flesh, and it needs to be treated as an evanescent thing, to be accepted as it is in the moment and never confined to our expectations. Simply allow the image of the spirit's face to come, and transfer that image back to the spirit, outside of yourself in the world of the real.

Take a moment before continuing to view the whole entity that you are observing. You have built a mental and a visual image of it from what you have received through your natural senses. Move your attention away from yourself, away from your mind, as your focus has surely shifted from the spirit to yourself, to your faulty imagination and your egoistic pride, and back to that space that was originally uncovered as being occupied by the spirit. Return your senses to the awareness of the reality of its presence, and now you do not have to simply understand that it is in that place, but you can see it standing there as you have analyzed its form. An interesting occurrence that is noted is that the spirit will seem to be suspended in time and space, allowing you to view it. In the realm of spirit, however, time and space do not exist as concrete laws, but are constructs of the mind, which are at times convenient, and at other times a nuisance. Do not allow the seeming suspension of the spirit to deter you from viewing it and from sensing its presence. Be sure, however, that the image that you are viewing is not in your mind, but is in the Temple, outside of yourself. Be honest with yourself and you will have little difficulty in trusting yourself.

Ask, "What does the spirit wear?" The image will be added to automatically. You may likewise ask yourself any question that will assist in the unveiling of the spirit.

The final question that you should ask for this exercise is not one for yourself alone, but is for both you and for the spirit. Sense the spirit there, and see it in your mental vision as you have uncovered it. Breathe in and feel the power that still floods through you reactivating within your chest. Let your breath out by asking, "Spirit, what you say?"

Initially the voice of the spirit will seem garbled or nonsensical. Relax your mind and feel the pressure that has gathered around your head, specifically around your ears. Feel it throbbing with a beat that may seem chaotic, much in the same way that words would seem were they not understood by other people of the same tongue. The words spoken by the spirit in response to the question will remain in the air around you. Relax your neck, your forehead, your ears, your eyes, your eyebrows, and your mind, and ask yourself, "What has the spirit said." The words may come slowly to you, one at a time until you grasp each. Allow them to come as they will, and if it is necessary, write them on a piece of paper as they come. One of the most difficult parts of this whole process of communicating with spirits is to hear the voice and for that voice to be heard in "real-time." Often, at first, the spirit's mouth will move and seconds later the first of a string of words will enter your mind. As you progress at hearing the voice and interpreting the words in your own native language, words will appear in your mind, and then the spirit will move its mouth to speak them. This is an inconsistency only in your observation, and with time and practice will balance itself out.

This whole process of viewing a spirit will likely span more than one viewing, but will require a persistent returning to the Temple, calling out to the spirits, and observing through the above steps. Sometimes the same spirit will appear, but other times it will not. The process does not change, nor does your ability to observe the spirit through your mind. All that will change is the image of the spirit if it is indeed one that you have not previously viewed, and the solidity and intensity of your observations. Once you have been able to completely view a spirit in one sitting through the above process, the time has come for you to take a field-trip. Go somewhere in nature, where all that can be seen is the earth and all that can be heard is the life that is all around. Seat yourself, not on a lawn chair that you have brought with you for comfort, but upon the hard ground or on a rock or tree stump, and go through the exact same steps of calling and of observation. Returning to the Temple each day, or removing yourself to some other place and observing spirits in this manner will begin to have a seemingly miraculous effect: the steps of visualization will come naturally, the questions will be answered before they are asked, and the images of the spirits will become more pronounced and concrete. Because you have called them near and have not called them forth, it is extremely rare for these wandering spirits to take on a form that is beholdable to the physical eyes, but your Greater Sight will be opened, and you will be ready to see and to hear any spirit that you wish to evoke to full manifestation.

Chapter Five
Basic Evocation

The authors of a majority of the workbooks, guidebooks, and grimoires of evocation have seemingly put their greatest efforts towards confusing the whole subject, the nature of which is amazingly simple once it has been successfully Worked following the basic principles and guidelines to achieve a consistent, reproducible, verifiable result. Most of these authors have restricted themselves to one or at most a few similar occult systems, as well as restricting themselves to what those systems define as good and evil, right and wrong, logical and insane, plausible and impossible. Man, by his very nature, is without limits or restrictions, and when he unites with the undying and unfaltering Powers of Magick, without fear or doubt, the Throne of God is just the beginning of his potential.

Because of these erroneous teachings, however, as well as his own belief that he does not possess the innate power to summon a spirit or the natural faculties to communicate with it, the Neophyte enters the Temple of evocation with the expectation of failing. I hear often as I teach these Arts that, "I've attempted several evocations, but none of them *worked*!"

My first follow-up question is, "Why not?" which usually provokes stammering followed by silence. My second question is, "How can you say with a certainty that the spirit did not hear your call, draw near, and wait for you to bring it into materialization?"

Again, silence. "Now, as you've repeated your attempts at evocation, what have you done differently to achieve the success that has eluded you?" This last question is usually answered with noncommittal, vague, emotional alterations that have supposedly been made to the ritual of evocation, such as, "I tried to *feel* the spirit more intensely when I called its name," or, "I really put my heart into it the last few times."

The spirits, demons, angels, elementals, jinn, and all of the countless other entities that can be summoned DO exist, independent of you and your desire to materialize them. When you call them in accordance with the elementary principles of evocation, they DO answer, regardless of whether you hang your head in defeat before the conjuration has even been recited to completion. If the spirit does not materialize in a manner that the Evocator can behold, such an assumed failure is due to the Neophyte's neglect of those simple and basic fundamentals that guarantee success. In nearly every case, the evocation has not failed at all, but the Summoner has failed to recognize the value of the thing that stands within the Temple waiting to be commanded, or the success of the Operation was abandoned in the first ten minutes of the ritual. Never does this ritual that has been used successful throughout millennia fail because the Evocator cannot pronounce a barbarous word correctly or because he has not spent enough time staring into empty space or into a glass ball or mirror to prepare himself.

Almost as often as students have approached me with reports of failed evocation, I have received reports from these same students of supernatural occurrences in their lives shortly after such "failures." The demons, which they attempted to summon, would begin manifesting in their lives, not as a spectral figure in the Triangle, but as an unstoppable force rearranging reality, trying desperately to fulfill the purpose of their being Called. The evocations being abandoned to failure, the Summoned would rarely grant the unspoken wishes of my students, but would find other ways by which they might influence their lives... usually leaving their default victims running to me for temporal salvation.

From the moment that you decide to perform an evocation, you *must* treat it as successful until you receive your end result. Never leave the ritual half-finished with demons lingering nearby waiting for your command. If you cannot sense the nearness of the Summoned when you have consecrated its sigil, center yourself, regain your focus, and begin again. If you are not able to see it when you have called it into full manifestation, calm your mind and emotions, refocus your will, attune your senses, and command it once more. This art of evocation is perhaps the most delicate science ever studied and ever put into practice since the beginning. The principles by which it functions, which have been applied consistently despite tradition or religion, and which have been outlined in this text, are the parameters of the equation, and once they are put into place will quantify themselves.

Preparing the Temple

The physical preparations of the Temple and tools are to be made no more than twelve hours and no less than one hour from the pre-appointed time of evocation. This will not only allow you to take your time and care in the arrangements, but also hallows that space and that day, with a certain knowledge of the hour of the Summoning.

If the Temple is indoors, it should be cleaned, swept, and picked up. If it is outdoors, all rocks, twigs, and debris are to be cleared from the area. I'm always amazed when I notice a particular Sorceress who I know rushes to scrub her home from ceiling to floor when her parents come to visit, but simply moves the clutter in the Temple away from the Circle and kicks some garbage away from the Triangle to prepare for a visitation from a Goetic King, an Archangel, or a Grand Demon.

Once your working area is clean, set out the Circle or Mandala that you have chosen to use, giving it at least a three-foot diameter. Directly outside of the Circle should be drawn, engraved, or in any other way impressed upon the physical ground an equilateral triangle, one of its points touching the circumference of the Circle and the other two creating a line parallel to the diameter of the Circle. The evocation and materialization is most phenomenal when the Triangle is placed in a cardinal direction most suitable to the nature of the Summoned. Often a planetary or elemental concordance is given for each spirit in its grimoire, and such can be used to position the Triangle accordingly:

Cardinal Direction	Element	Planetary Influence
North	Earth	Moon, Neptune, Uranus
East	Air	Mercury, Venus
West	Water	Saturn, Jupiter
South	Fire	Mars, Sun

The Archangels Raphael, Michael, Gabriel, and Auriel are called from their respective positions, Raphael to the east, Michael to the south, Gabriel to the west, and Auriel to the North, and their familiars may be called from the same direction. Elemental spirits are to be called facing the cardinal direction correlating with the spirit's element. More generically, and less "properly," angels are to be evoked with the Triangle in the east, demons in the south, spirits of the dead in the west, and intelligences in the north.

Place a brazier in the center of the Triangle of Manifestation, filled with fresh coal. Avoid the temptation to purchase special incense coal disks from the local pagan peddler. These are usually too small to be effective for burning the amount of incense needed for evocation, too awkwardly shaped to pile together, and they burn too quickly without giving off enough heat to smolder the whole of the incense quickly. Incense is used in evocation not primarily for the scent, but for the smoke. There are several theories that postulate as to the exact mechanism of the incense smoke in evocation and full materialization, from providing a thick yet malleable substance with which the spirit may build a body to causing a unique type of carbon-monoxide asphyxiation, which releases endorphins, and dopamine that in turn results in the hallucination of the spirit. Pools of fresh blood are also used in more extreme and demonic forms of evocation, usually with greater success than the intoxicating smoke. Again, the explanations range from ectoplasmic dispersal from the blood to the psychological impact of such a gruesome presence that causes the Evocator to view and hear the evoked. Is it so far away from the realm of believability and experience of those that summon forth demonic legions or angelic armies for the purposes of realigning fate that perhaps the incense, warm blood, semen, or the other materials used for the manifestation of the spirit possess a virtue in and of themselves which alter the immediate area to allow for spiritual materialization?

Some traditionalists insist that the brazier must be held under cold, purified water to be cleansed of spiritual impurity, and must be consecrated with the other ritual tools. The function of the brazier, however, is a physical rather than a spiritual one. It is placed in the Triangle so that the incense may smolder without burning the entire Temple to the ground.

A supply of incense is to be kept within the Circle, as it will be continuously heaped upon the burning brazier through-out the ritual. Most Operations of evocation will require a large amount of incense to be burned, so although custom incense can be expensive, take care to have more than enough lest you run out of your materialization base while the demon is midway through formation. Sandalwood, frankincense, and Dittany of Crete have been used for centuries in evocation, and have proven their worth for nearly every practicing Sorcerer. It may be advantageous, however, to choose incense that directly coincides with the sphere of origin of the entity that you will be calling, or often working off of intuition or True Vision alone will produce unparalleled results. While Frankincense is excellent for the evocation of Raphael, it is sandalwood that will allow a more full materialization of most elemental spirits, and modern Dragon's Blood incense works well with most minor Goetic entities. In the same vein, you can burn sage picked straight from the brush for the evocation of spirits of wisdom or peace if you happen to live in the desert, or you can heap dry human hair onto the coals to create a noxious smoke that will materialize most any Qlippothic or truly demonic entity.

Your altar should be set in the exact center of the Circle, and upon it should sit either two black or two white candles. Multicolored candles rarely provide enough added energy or "feeling" to an evocation to make it worthwhile, and usually will lend more towards a distracting hobby of candle selection. Simple black or simple white will suffice. A rule of thumb in preparation for evocation is that the Triangle, its contents, and the visible Circle are there for the Summoned. Everything within the Triangle is there for you. The focus of the ritual of evocation is not you, the object, but is the spirit that you wish to call, the subject, and so the bulk of the pretty, shining colors and decorative arrangements should be consigned to the circumference of the Circle or to the area of the

Triangle. In effect, despite having a Circle made of fire or colored riverbed stone, or any other display, and even though the Triangle may contain the most ornate script in existence to seal it up, as well as a century-old brazier in which the incense is to be burned, the inside of the Circle – the area in which you, the Evocator, Operate – is to remain entirely bland. All objects upon the altar are to be functional. The white or black candles serve to illuminate the immediate area, the chalice holds the wine and is the receptive end of the energy of the ritual, and the ritual dagger directs the will of the Sorcerer, and may at times be used to cut.

The two candles are to be set at the left and right edges of the altar. The chalice is set to left of the altar to the inside of the candle, and is to be half-filled with wine, meade, water, or blood. The dagger is to be placed likewise to the right, its sharp point towards the Triangle. A journal should be present on the altar, in which the details of the evocation may be recorded immediately after the dismissal of the entity, as well as any specific instructions given by the Summoned spirit. While in the majority it is far better to have the whole of the Operation from start to finish committed to memory, for the purpose of your first few evocation rituals, you may take into the Circle notes that you have made, or even this entire book. Whatever you choose, you must have a bound notebook or guidebook rather than a loose sheet of notepaper. The final object to set upon the altar is the sigil of the spirit, drawn on a five inch square piece of paper or parchment, laid facing down on the altar.

In traditional evocation, the Summoner will be usually be armed with a ritual sword, which acts in a similar manner as the dagger but can be extended *outside* of the Circle. Such a tool is advantageous when the incense in the brazier begins to wane, allowing the Magician to place a pile of resin on the flat of the blade, reach into the center of the Triangle of Manifestation, and dump the powder onto the coals. Avoiding the superfluous, however, there is no need to purchase or manufacture a ritual sword and consecrate it to the Great Art when its only function is to transport incense from the Circle to the brazier – assuming that the Operator has evolved beyond the belief that in order to enlist the aide of an entity whose very nature is to carry out the task set before it that it must be beaten into coercion and threatened with a Divine Authority which most of these ritual bullies don't possess in the first place. A slat of metal or even wood can easily be used for the purpose of moving incense, as well as a plethora of pre-manufactured devices designed specifically for this task!

Returning to the Temple at the appointed time, your first task will be the consecration of all Magickal devices that will be used to bring about the evocation of the chosen entity. This consecration will set apart each device in your mind as having importance in the ritual, as well as imbuing the physical matter with actual, tangible spiritual significance. Nearly every system of evocation outside of the one presented here demands that each ritual tool be consecrated shortly after it is procured, wrapped in black silk or some other fabric, and put away until the time of the evocation. I have found time and again that if the tools of Magick are consecrated and set apart during an actual ritual intended to bring actual results, the consecration will have a more realistic effect on both the tools and the Operator than if they are charged with power in a ritual that has no real-world purpose. The whole act of Magick is to bring that which exists in the realms and states beyond the flesh through the veils of vision and touch into the real, solid world. No other ritual exemplifies this doctrine more than that of evocation to physical materialization. Even in Ascent, the Sorcerer is not raising himself to a higher level or plane of existence, but is reaching into his own inner Godhood and bringing that into the present and physical being, allowing his latent autonomy to erupt from within him. Buying a hammer, knowing deep within yourself that it is a hammer, imagining the houses that the hammer will build, and pretending to slam nails into lumber does absolutely no good. The hammer is only a tool when it is used as such. Otherwise, it is a lump of metal attached to a stick.

Stand behind the altar facing the direction from which you will call the spirit forth. Perform the Invocation of Omnipotence as given in Chapter Three, holding the omnipotent force inside of yourself rather than breathing it out. Lay your palms upon the altar, your wrists, and your fingers relaxed, and close your eyes. Bring into your inner vision the image of the altar, feeling it beneath your fingers and seeing it clearly in your mind. The floor and walls of the Temple are unimportant, as are the objects upon the altar. Inhale, feeling the bright omnipotence within you stir, feeling your torso and your arms and your hands tingling with the electricity that is about to flow through them. Hold the breath for a moment and sense the radiance filling your chest, ready to explode into the world. Release the air through your mouth and simultaneously release as much of the power within you through your hands into the altar. Feel the bone, muscle, and flesh on your arms and hands parting, giving way to the unearthly force flowing through you. Sense the cold, hard matter beneath your fingers coming to life. Visualize it glowing with the same brightness that is within and around you. As the light leaves you, know that it is instantly regenerated, your body becoming an eternal fountain of power. Allow this power to continue flooding from you into the altar, bringing to startling life its every molecule.

If you have mastered and grown comfortable with the exercise for invoking omnipotence, the flow of dynamic, creative and assertive power will not need to be forced or imagined in any way, but will flood through you without restraint the moment that you will it to be.

When the altar will accept no more power and light, inhale and feel the flow of tangible omnipotence ceasing, the energy moving from your hands to your arms, and finally returning to the storehouse within your torso. Look down at the altar and see the Divine glow emanating from it, the granules of its composition all singing with life. Before you sever the connection between your hands and the altar, seal the power and light within it, so that its ever fiber will contain the omnipotence long after it has crumbled into dust. Inhale, regain your focus upon the altar, and state in a clear, smooth voice, "Creation of (stone/wood/plastic), be the altar and the foundation upon which my universe will be brought up into existence. I seal this calling upon you, and I seal the power to perform your function within you, Eternal." See in your inner vision the light and the power that you have filled the altar with solidifying, becoming a thing of this physical plane rather than an abstract spiritual idea. Sense the luminescence merging with the molecules of the altar, the object no longer being simply physical, yet at the same time not being purely spiritual, but instead a union between the upper and the lower.

The same transfer of power and purpose is to be made with the chalice first, cradling the bowl of it in both hands and breathing life into the metal. Call, "Creation of brass/silver/tin, be the chalice which holds the power of the Operations of Magick within you and offers the waters of life to the lips of the worthy. I seal this calling upon you, and I seal the power to perform your function within you, Eternal." Visualize the power being sealed within the molecules of the metal and set the chalice down in its place and take the ritual dagger in your right hand. Clasping both your right hand and the dagger in your left hand, point skywards, hold the dagger a few inches from your sternum and begin infusing it with the omnipotent force within you. When it is brimming with power, call, "Creation of steel, be the dagger through which the will and power of Magick may flow and cause change in this world. I seal this calling upon you, and I seal the power to perform your function within you, Eternal." Visualize the power and purpose being sealed within the steel, and lower the dagger to your side in your right hand.

Walk to the Triangle of Manifestation and, beginning at the point nearest the Circle, trace the outline of the Triangle. Feel the force within you traveling down your arm, through your hand, filling the dagger and leaving its tip in the form of a fiery light. At the point of the dagger passes over the lines, visualize them glowing red, as if a line of spiritual fire has replaced the drawn lines. If you have engraved characters or images within the Triangle, these do not need to be traced. When you have returned to the original point, hold the dagger at your side in your left hand and stretch out your right hand over that point. See in your inner vision the glowing red Triangle that you have drawn in the spiritual world. Sense its purpose of providing a place wherein the spirit may manifest. State, "Creation of Magick, be the Triangle of Manifestation in which the spirit (spirit's name) will materialize before me when called. Hold within you the elements and forces required of (spirit's name) to manifest in a beholdable form before me. I seal this calling upon you, and I seal the power to perform your function within you, Eternal."

Before you leave the Triangle, light the coals within the brazier, readying them for the incense.

Taking the dagger again in your right hand, move to the inside of the Circle, touching the point of it that connects with the Triangle with the tip of the dagger. Again channel power through the dagger, emitting a fiery blue energy as it leaves the blade and touches the ground. This can also be visualized as an indigo flame that burns on the ground touched by the dagger's blade. Holding the tip of the dagger to the drawn Circle, move diesel (clockwise or "sun wise") for angelic, benevolent, or altruistic entities, or move widdershins (counterclockwise) for demonic, malign, or baneful entities, tracing an "astral double" of the Circle's perimeter in the fiery blue light. Again, if you have decided to use an elaborate mandala all that is necessary to trace is the most basic figure of the Circle. When you have returned to the Circle's point of origin, hold the tip of the dagger on that point which connects the Circle to itself and again to the Triangle, and call, "Creation of Art, be the Circle in which the Eternal is made manifest now and in which all things formed and unformed, past and future are brought into present reality. I seal this calling upon you, and I seal the power to perform your function within you, Eternal." Visualize the melding of the spiritual blue fire with the Circle that you have drawn on the ground.

Return to your place behind the altar, set the dagger in its place, and look out upon the Circle and the Triangle. With your eyes open and your Vision active, see the red glow of the Triangle and know its purpose. See the burning indigo Circle and know its function. Take a deep breath in and feel in your core the reality of these two images that you have consecrated. Look down at the altar, the chalice, and the dagger, and see them aglow with the life that you have given them. Look inside of yourself and feel the Divine Power within still radiating, still glowing with the brightness of a million suns, still ready to pour its power into the universe.

Take the chalice in your left hand, the cup of it cradled in your fingers, and rest its base on the center of the altar, keeping your left hand under it. See the light that has been sealed into the altar rising up like steam to warm the liquid in the chalice, climbing up the stem like ivy. Hold your right hand over the mouth of the chalice, your index, and middle fingers extended. Inhale and gather the omnipotence within yourself into your torso. Exhale and begin pushing it through your right arm, into your hand, and feel and see it filling those two outstretched fingers, the brightness of the light of life resting on the tips of your fingers, threatening to burst the flesh and escape like a river into the chalice. Inhale, feeling the power in your fingers and the well of energy behind it growing, dip your fingers in the wine, exhale, and release the omnipotence into the liquid. Look into the chalice and see the wine becoming infused with power. Feel it warming to the touch, all of the power of God trapped within this fluid. When the wine has taken in all of the energy it can hold, keeping your fingers in the wine, call, "Creation of the vine, be the elixir which will make this flesh immortal, be the blood of God which will purify this Soul, be the nectar which will awaken this mind, be the waters which will bring absolution. I seal this calling upon you, and I seal the power to perform your function within you, Eternal."

While the primary function of this consecration rite, which is to be performed at the beginning of each and every evocation ritual, is to set the items and ritual devices apart with Magickal power and spiritual purpose, its secondary and more covert function is to bring about the full attainment of omnipotence. In the uniquely short amount of time taken to consecrate each object, to draw the Triangle and the Circle in fiery light, and to charge the liquid within the chalice, while your environment changes and takes on a true spiritual form, you yourself also are being transmuted, standing again behind the altar not as a human capable of doubting that which you are about to do and about to see, but as a Divine Being who knows that the powers and energies that circle around you and fill every line and object within the Temple are capable of doing nothing but bringing to full manifestation the spirit that you are about to call.

Most Practitioners at this point, depending on the particular system from which they Work, will either begin calling incantations, conjurations, and constraints that will "force" the spirit to appear, or they will forego these orations and immediately attempt to connect with the spirit through its sigil. In order to establish the needed substantial connection – a connection that by far surpasses the enviable human intellect and consciousness – a deal of grace and delicacy needs to be balanced with a firm assertion of your will. Leave the chalice in the center of the altar, as you will be drinking the sacred liquid from it momentarily, and place the sigil of the spirit face-up on the altar. Gaze it at for a moment, knowing that it is the symbol that will link you to none other than the spirit that you are going to call into materialization before you. Look up towards the Triangle, in the empty space above the drawn image where the spirit will soon occupy, and state, "(Spirit's name), hear my voice, see my signs, and know that I command the universe to bring you before me, so that I may see you, so that I may hear you, and so that your power will be my power, your strength will be my strength, and your knowledge will be my knowledge." With the same two fingers that were dipped into the wine, touch the face of the spirit's sigil, imparting the same energy, filling the fibers of the paper with light, and say, "I seal this calling upon you, and I seal the power to perform this feat within this Temple in which you will manifest."

This initial oration affirms in your mind that you are not *requesting* the assistance of the spirit, nor are you leaving its manifestation to debate, but that it is a reality, and that it has been sealed to come to pass. At the same time, you are not yet commanding *the spirit* to appear, but are instead commanding the universe to bring the spirit into appearance, and commanding the Temple to be the place in which it will materialize. Few Sorcerers, in their first evocations, are able to fathom the fact that because of their very nature as Ascendant beings destined for Godhood, they are capable of having power over a timeless, seemingly invincible demon or archangel. They *can*, however believe that through their Magick they have control over their environment, which in their Neophytic minds is inanimate. Therefore, they erroneously believe that if they command the spirit, the spirit can refuse; if they command the universe at large, and the Temple in specific, however, these "reactive" organisms will respond unfailingly.

At the calling of the spirit's name, in such an omnipotent state of being and with all of the Magickal devices in place, the spirit will indeed hear your voice and see your signs, the fullness of its attention moving towards the Temple, the Circle, and the Triangle of Manifestation, and as the connection made with the entity grows increasingly more substantial, it will draw nearer not only to the location of the Temple, but will also descend from its ethereal abode through veils of materialization until it stands on this earth in a form that is undeniably real.

It is also at this point in the ritual of evocation that lightheadedness, physical exhaustion, and general weariness will begin to manifest. At first, the Evocator will fear that he does not possess the natural stamina to complete the ritual, or will be hounded by the anxiety that in such a state he will not be able to wrestle with the spirit for control. This state of decided weakness is often referred to as "Magickal fatigue," is a normal and necessary stage of evocation, and can usually be taken as a sign of the oncoming materialization of the spirit. As far as the latter fear: there is no need to wrestle with any entity for control, be it the angel of mercy or the demon of pestilence. It is not by the power of the human being who weakens under the force of omnipotence, who becomes ill when disease enters his blood, who must be sustained by eating, drinking, sleeping, and defecating, who will eventually wither, die, and decay, it is not by this being that miracles are brought about, but it is through the power of the God within which is by nature omnipresent, omnipotent, omniscient, who never weakens and never dies that the spirit is brought into manifestation, that it is constrained to do the will of the Sorcerer, that it is obedient to the oaths that it makes, and that the whole of the heavens part when commanded by the voice of the Divine, issued from the lips of the human that trembles behind the altar.

The state of weakness can be more appropriately called a state of rapture. The body is being transfigured, prepared by a power that is beyond the flesh to see and hear, that which is also beyond the flesh. The mild exhaustion, which you feel at this point early on in the ritual, will increase as the ritual progresses and as the spirit moves closer to materialization within the Triangle. Do not fight it, as in doing so you will be fighting the very thing that will lift you from your dying state into one of Godly power, but instead give into the exhaustion. Allow it to overwhelm you. As the ritual moves forward and the rapture grows more fervent, you may begin to feel as if you are near complete conscious collapse and will faint at any moment. You must walk the line between the blackness of unconsciousness and the willed command over your own body, giving up your will to do anything at all but to remain alert. If your knees are locked, unlock them and loosen your stance. Control your breath, focus your mind, and continue the ritual.

Still looking towards the empty space within the Triangle, raise the chalice above your head, the base of it level with your forehead, and say, "I drink the blood of God. I take within me all of His/Her/Its power." Drink some of the wine within the chalice, feeling the energy that has been infused in the fluid refreshing the omnipotence within you, reawakening your senses and bringing your whole being back to life. Put the chalice back in its place on the left hand of the altar. Using either a ritual sword if you have chosen such a tool or the metal or wood slat, pour a good deal of incense on the hot coals, creating a large amount of smoke in the Triangle. Place your hands, palms down on the altars surface, each one on either side of the sigil. Gaze down at the sigil, take a deep breath in, and allow your vision to relax so that you are not staring *at* the drawing, but rather seem to be looking *through* it. As you let the breath out, feel your mind connecting with the mind of the spirit that lingers nearby, waiting to be called into manifestation. Before anything whatsoever can be brought into fruition, it must first be brought into mind in a clear image of what is desired. As you gaze at the sigil, bring to mind the purpose for which you are performing the ritual of evocation. Try to focus your thoughts on this goal as a single image of that which you desire, rather than a random assortment of feelings and wishes. Decide exactly what it is that you want, and see that thing in your mind. As your mental image sharpens, feel the impending reality of achieving it. Do not wish for it any longer, but *know* that it is being brought to you in that very moment. As you do this, sense the raw force of this desire and the knowledge of its attainment seeping from your mind into the sigil; a transfer that is uniquely automatic. As the energy fills the paper, the lines of ink will first "feel" as if they are coming to life. They will course with an energy that will soon become visible. Often, the first sign of the full connection with the sigil is the disappearance of a section of ink from your vision. A line, a portion of the surrounding circle, or a smaller internal symbol will "jump" out of your vision, and will return seconds later, usually seeming to no longer rest on the paper, but instead float above it. It is important that you not allow your vision to focus on the one section that has disappeared, but to instead view the whole image at once. In doing so, another section will disappear and return in vibrant life, until the whole sigil has followed cue.

You will notice after this process has completed that the spirit whose sigil you are charging is much more near than before. Those Sorcerers who have been blessed or cursed with natural clairvoyance will often hear the voice of the spirit announcing its presence, or will begin to see the room visibly changing, growing darker or lighter, becoming warmer, or taking on a different hue. If this happens, which will occur increasingly with each evocation, do not assume that the spirit is present in its fullness and that you can begin striking deals and issuing commands. The spirit is never to be considered manifest until you can see it in the Triangle and until its mouth moves and its words fill the air.

If the smoke from the brazier is waning, add more incense, return to your stance behind the altar, and gaze again at the sigil. Even though your eyes have departed from it, it should still pulse with the energy that you have given it, and the spirit will still be known to be near. Pull your gaze from the sigil to the space in the Triangle where the cloud of smoke drifts upwards, inhale deeply and feel the presence of the spirit moving closer to that space that has been set aside and sealed up for its materialization. Bring your mind and your physical vision into the same state of awareness that has been cultivated by viewing wandering spirits, and with that Vision awakened look into the Triangle. It is at this juncture that the actual materialization of the spirit will commence, and despite the claims of Hollywood and a good deal of modern occult advisors, this process takes at best a few minutes, the entire atmosphere of the Temple converting to accommodate the presence of the spirit, the particles of air thickening, the physical illumination changing, the matter making up the walls, floor, and ceiling being transfigured to accept the full manifestation of impossibility in tangible form.

As the evidence hitherto has pointed out, the main body of occult Practitioners is often divided in dual parts, and the materialization of the spirit is no exception. One hand states with full confidence and supposed authority that the manifestation of the spirit is not in actuality physical, that the spirit instead connects with the Evocator in such a substantial degree that the Magician can see so clearly in his mind an image of the spirit that it seems real and physical. The other hand affirms that the spirit does manifest physically, often accompanied by physical phenomenon which can be observed and recorded by absolutely anyone despite previous preparation, as well as certain visual and auditory phenomenon, such as the sound of frantic pounding on the walls of the Temple, loud vocal emissions coming from nowhere, erratic lights, and even brightly colored figures, embodiments, or shapes appearing. In the first few years of my experience and experiments with evocation, I sided with the former school, having evoked and communicated with spirits mainly through a scrying mirror, and when I did manage to evoke to full physical materialization, days later my objective mind would convince my higher understanding that the whole thing had been a projection of my brain and my expectations. Aside from the appearance of the spirit that I was calling, I had never noticed any other phenomenon, and was certain that those claiming to have seen and heard such things were merely elaborating their stories for reaction and attention.

In the winter of 2002 I traveled to the seemingly one place on earth that sunshine and happiness had forsaken, Wisconsin, to teach in person these delicate Works to one of my more promising students. I planned to stay and train him in the most basic facets of the occult for at least a year, and we decided the he, his wife (who had no interest in the occult at all), and I would rent a house together for the time that I would be with him. In the two-story house that we rented, I took the upstairs and the couple stayed in the downstairs area. Once we had settled in and became comfortable with the arrangement, I set up my Temple in an empty room and began Working in it. After about a month of living together, studying, and putting into practice the principles of the occult arts with my student, I found myself in need of bringing about the full physical evocation of a specific, very powerful entity. I made the proper arrangements and returned to the Temple at twilight that night. I began the ritual in the manner set forth above, burned large quantities of incense, charged the sigil, called forth the entity through the appropriate conjuration, and as it materialized in the room, I heard my student's wife downstairs yell in a forcedly loud voice, "God damn it! Knock it off!" Her husband was working the night shift at a convenience store, so either she was taking with herself, or she was yelling at me. I had spoken the conjuration out loud, but not by any means loudly. I had actually restrained my voice and my actions with the knowledge that she was home, as to not make any disturbing noise whatsoever.

I returned my attention to the evocation, and continued bringing the spirit into manifestation, this time being sure to not make any clamor that might disturb my housemate. The moment that the spirit was plainly in view and I greeted it, I heard my student's wife shouting profanations once more, this time thundering up the stairs full of grumbles and annoyance at me for some unknown reason. She rapped on my door as heavily as she could manage, and I quickly dismissed the spirit and closed the ritual. I swung open the door, filled with wrath, and saw my student's wife on the other side fuming, her face red, and her eyes bulging.

"What the hell do you think you're doing? You could have a little respect for those of us who work in the morning!" I was speechless, without a clue as to what she meant. Furthermore, I too had a job to attend in the morning.

"What's the problem," I finally managed to get out. She noticed my genuinely confused expression and tried to simmer as much of her rage down as possible.

"I'm trying to sleep, and all I can hear is you pounding on the walls, stomping on the floor, yelling, and whatever lights that you've got on flashing through the whole house!" I was more confused than I had been when I opened the door.

"I was in here performing a ritual, but I know that I was being quiet, and I definitely was *not* pounding walls or thumping floors." She glared at me and stomped back down the stairs to her bedroom.

When my student returned home, we sat in our living room and discussed the incident. I was apologetic, but for what I wasn't exactly sure.

"What kind of ritual were you doing?" he asked.

"An evocation," I replied, not quite seeing the connection.

"And do you think that whatever it was that you were calling up could have made the racket?"

I sat silent, pondering the possibility that perhaps something real and something physical *did* materialize in that house, and if so, why was I not aware of the excess phenomena? And if indeed phenomena did follow evocation, and for whatever reason I was not privy to seeing and hearing it, have walls been pounded, ceilings been thumped upon, voices been shouted from nowhere, and lights been flashed from the vacuous air every time, unbeknownst to me?

Because of that incident, I have gone back to performing my rituals far from the eyes and ears of others, and today, my Temple is in a cave in the side of a mountain, and when I evoke the spirit will take on its usual solid form. The wind might blow a bit harder than before or thunder might roll through the sky in coincidence with the appearance of the spirit, but aside from the image of the spirit before me and the sound of the words that it speaks, I see no flashing lights and I hear no bumps in the night, and there is no one around to tell me differently.

The one separation I can find between those that do experience these odd phenomena and those that simply see the one thing that they have set out to see is the ritual approach to evocation and the preparation of the Evocator. Often, those experiencing phenomena will enter a ritual with a "let's see what happens" attitude, or with the perception that the whole Operation is out of his or her hands and is at the will and wish of the spirit. Their focal points are few, if they have any at all, and they simply perform the ritual, following the basic principles of evocation, and wait for something to happen - and often something does. Those who see nothing but the spirit and hear nothing but its voice usually enter the Temple with a sure expectation of what they will see and how the whole Operation will turn out. They go into the thing as a scientific procedure that can have only one outcome if all of the correct principles are applied, and that is indeed the outcome that they find.

Whether you hear pounding on the walls and see flashing lights, if the spirit's voice enters your mind or drifts through the air, or if the incense smoke simply seems to suspend in air and wrap tightly around the center of the Triangle, maintain your focus and your purpose. Inhale slowly and deeply and sense the spirit in the same way that you have sensed spirits in your previous exercises. Relax your mind and allow it to find the location of the spirit that you are Summoning, which should be taking form in the Triangle. If it is not, but rather wanders the room, try not to turn your attention to it, but remain concentrated on the Triangle and the drifting incense smoke. Sense the internal connection between your mind and will and that of the spirits as surely as any concrete thing, and using that connection, "will" the spirit to enter the Triangle. The key here is not to attempt to force with your thoughts or feelings the spirit to do any one thing, but rather to release your desire and your doubt and to *know* that the spirit moves towards the Triangle. From the core of your being, wherein the One True God resides, will the spirit toward the Triangle. You will enter a type of meditative or Gnostic state in doing so, the rapture that had previously crept upon you growing fierce, yet a unique type of control also being present and undeniable.

As this silent and passive assertion of will is taking place, with your eyes still locked on the smoke, recite the conjuration that will call the spirit into manifestation. Inhale, allow the Magickal fatigue and rapture to swoon you as much as it will, reawaken your awareness of the omnipotence that is within you, feel it flowing up your throat and spilling from your lips by the words of the conjuration.

"(Spirit's name), I call you and conjure you forth to stand in this Temple and to take your place within the Triangle. I summon you to manifest before me in beholdable form and to speak with me in a discernable voice. (Spirit's name), I give you license to appear, I give you power to manifest, I give you this call to come. (Spirit's name), come!"

After this simple conjuration is given, the spirit will immediately begin to materialize, which often will not be an instantaneous process. As it moves through the worlds of energy and spirit towards the realm of flesh, the physical makeup of the Temple will change more dramatically, the air thickening, the lights either dimming or growing brighter, and the rapture that has been taking you will reach a dizzying peak. While reality adjusts to make way for the Summoned, do not break your attention and your will from the Triangle, and repeat in a hushed voice, "(Spirit's Name), come!"

The psychological result of the Operation thus far, with the atmospheric and environmental shifts, the culminating spiritual exhaustion, the force of the spirit's arrival itself, and the constant flow of omnipotence through you will be either one of startling revelation, seeing through the fog that threatens to extinguish consciousness the image of the spirit building in the smoke, or of an often more intense experience of the whole self sinking beneath the causal world, falling into the underworld and its nihilistic trance as if through fiery rings of reality until you find that the spirit is so close that it could be touched if you dared, could be ingested with a breath, standing in its fullness in the center of the Triangle, a guest in this world awaiting its host's welcome.

Do not judge the vision, in whatever manner it shows itself. The spirit has appeared before you, and you can indeed see it, hear it, smell the effluence coming from its freshly materialized skin – you have in every way called into full physical manifestation the spirit that you have summoned. Do not allow your brain to try to interpret the image or the functions of the senses; simply see, hear, and accept the power and the glory that has sealed the communion.

Welcome the Summoned briefly, yet graciously: "(Spirit's Name), I welcome you to this Temple, and I thank you eternally for answering my call and for your swift and full attendance."

The Evoked will rarely reply, and those who do rarely do so in a polite manner. Do not be disconcerted by their silence or by their clamor, but move forward with the intent of the ritual: the issuance of the task.

"(Spirit's Name), it is my will that…" It is at this point that your desires are to be made known *precisely*. These spirits that you call are ancient, having watched every civilization rise from nothing and return to nothing, if not personally having a hand in the process. Most of the time, the Summoned will know why you have called it before the conjuration is even recited, and waits to be set loose upon the world to bring to pass your will by your command. Despite the admonitions of the pious, a Temple is not a place for guilt, shame, timidity, or ambiguity. Rather, it is the one space wherein you may stand and declare your place and claim your birthright as God of your world. The spirits will often be able to advise on the best course to take towards your goal, and if you plot with them, they will plot a route that will have no other possible end but the achievement of your goal.

When you have gained the information or provided a task, dismiss the spirit to do the work, or to return to its place of origin. With the final vestiges of the omnipotence within you, state, "(Spirit's Name), I thank you eternally for your attendance, and for the accomplishment of the tasks with which you have been charged. Go now into the world to bring to manifestation those things, armed with power and sealed with purpose. (Spirit's Name), you are dismissed." With this, the spirit's body will begin to dissipate. The Temple, however, will still hold to the environmental alterations that have been made, such as the light, the thickness of the air, etc. until such energies are exorcised or fade over time.

Only once in my career as an Evocator did the spirit not leave when dismissed, and such was indeed an occasion for immense anxiety. I had evoked a planetary spirit for assistance in the creation of a certain work of art, and although the nature of the spirit is known to be essentially benevolent, it also tends towards a childish guile, acting at times as the genius trickster. I gave the dismissal, yet it still stood in the Triangle armed with a boyish grin. I repeated the dismissal, and he still remained. This occurred within my first year of experience in evocation, and I was completely unprepared for the event. I stood in the Circle, terrified and confused, not knowing what could be done, and even more terrified of the possibility that the spirit may choose to never leave, and the harm that might come to me as a result. I finally flipped through the pages of the grimoire in which I had found the name and sigil of the spirit, and recited the banishing which succeeds the whole ritual, and the spirit then vanished. For good measure, I repeated the banishing, closed the ritual, and left the Circle. It took a few months after that occasion for me to dare to perform another evocation.

If you have chosen to perform a banishing after the ritual of evocation, rather than allowing the energy of the Working to dissipate on its own, or if the rare and unfortunate experience accounted above graces your Temple, the following banishing, taken from the recently translated grimoire Kingdoms of Flame[2], has always served me well. It must be spoken with authority, and with a sure knowledge of the potency of the words, the sound of which will cleanse the area of all energies whatsoever.

"Ashtu malku ta dat arkata
astus seckz altamu partu
Iretempal krez ta felta
Vaskalla regent met senturus
Ta sastrus estos melta
Kelta, kelta, ketla hine."

At the speaking of this exorcism, the apparent illumination and the composition of the air itself will lighten, and usually with no more than three repetitions, the Temple will be as it was before the evocation.

At the conclusion of a completely successful Operation of evocation, you will feel an immortal exhaustion, as if you could sleep for days. Ravenous hunger may also set in. For purposes of retraction, it is always better to satisfy your hunger before satisfying your tiredness, as to not allow your mind to move directly from the Godstate to the unconscious state, but to return to a state of normal functioning before anything else. Attempt to do something that will remove your mind from the previous hour entirely. Watching television or reading a book may not be the best options for retuning to a normal state, as both will allow you to drift from the show or the story, instead daydreaming about the face and the voice of the spirit, or the feeling of the Godlike power that moved through you. I have always preferred the company of other people directly following the company of undying beings as a perfect balance.

When you are able to think back to the evocation and the whole thing seems like an event remembered from a distant dream or a past life, you can be sure that your mind has returned to a state of normal operation, and you can also be sure that the spirit is able to work upon the world without any restraint from you. Although the novelty of the Operation will fade, and the reality of it may be questioned in the days and weeks following, each and every time that you return to the Temple, the spirits will fly at your command, and you will again stand atop that pyramid of skulls as God of your world.

As you find more spirits to evoke, and as your desires and problems in life grow increasingly more important and even Aeonic, you will often find that you naturally gravitate towards one or two specific types of entities. For quite a while, I worked with nothing but demons, and on a rare occasion that I had need to summon an angel, the feeling of the whole Operation was alien to me, not because the syntax had changed, but because in the company of demons, I myself had become in a manner of speaking, demonic. My thoughts, attitudes, and actions became increasingly darker, more sinister, and at the peak of my demonic communion, had become criminally malevolent. I also experienced a power and a superiority over the human race whom I viewed more and more as an alien species herded to an fro on this planet until their inevitable extinction by those of us that reigned. My mind was not functioning as a human's would have, but was instead peering through the collective vantage of the demons with which I surrounded myself. The orthodox explanation was obvious possession, or as Catholic Exorcists claimed, I was "perfectly possessed," entirely aware of the demonic influence within me, and completely accepting of that influence in my life.

Modern occultists separate the classical possession from the "demonic obsession" that can occur with evocation. The Evocator will become so infatuated with an entity or a type of entity that he will evoke nothing else, and will as a result saturate the whole of his being with the energies, thoughts, attitudes, and even familiars of those entities that he evokes. It is the old adage of surrounding yourself with people that you wish to become like, rather than surrounding yourself with those who wish to become like you.

While finding perfect balance is essential to Ascent, there is also much to be said for experiencing everything to its fullest, immersing oneself in darkness and evil to the point of oblivion, and then rising from the depth of Perdition into the glory and light envied by the angels, and moving from there into the middle path of exaltation beyond the flesh and above the throne of God. Most do lose themselves either in the darkness or the light, however, and never find that column of Light and sound which offers to carry them into the heart of the Eternal. There is only one entity in the whole of the universe that is capable of revealing your destiny, however, and the steps needed to walk towards it, and that entity is yourself. Make conscious decisions regarding which entities you will Work with.

Understand their nature and their intent, and evoke them knowing that as you do, you may find within yourself an familiarity with that spirit, and a desire to hold its power and knowledge for yourself, rather than relegating your tasks to the spirits. Become responsible, each time you enter your Temple, for the direction of your own spiritual motion, whether it is to the left, or to the right, towards heaven or hell, do not put your destiny in the hands of any but yourself.

Regardless of the specific entities that you choose to align yourself with, and resultantly choose to be more like, the greatest advice of the greatest Mages is to evoke often. Constantly surrounding yourself with that which you wish to emulate, you will gradually absorb more and more of their virtues, imbued with the very power that you are Summoning. Evoking the entities of your desire will also put into effect a certain compounded momentum. The spirits and their powers will remain active in your life, their familiars surrounding you and their energies effecting all around you. The force that is within you, and those forces that are without, will become active in the most spontaneous manner.

Part II - Aided Ascent

Chapter Six
Emissaries of Ascent

The ability to evoke to physical materialization any entity at will, to communicate with that spirit openly and to issue a command that it will utilize all of its influence, familiars, knowledge, and power to accomplish is one of the greatest landmarks of the Magician's Ascent towards Godhood. The Evocator quickly realizes that with the assistance of the darkest demons he is capable of swinging open the gates of hell on earth and unleashing apocalyptic devastation; that by summoning Archangels the kingdom of heaven in all of its peace and abundance will be brought to living glory on earth; that through materializing some of the most ancient spirits he can learn how to build an empire around him, and through evoking servitors his empire can be fortified for all time. If he employs the Operations given in the first part of this book, the needs of daily living are met almost instantaneously, and he finds himself looking towards the stars, wondering if he can reach them if he tries, or if he can pull them to earth if he puts forth his will. He is at home in a world that no longer seems to spin farther away from his control, but instead spins simply to allow him to learn more, to grow stronger, to become the God who looks back at him from the mirror.

Evocation has opened every door, unlocked every gate for his passing, and when he is ready it is this very tool that will allow him to take the final steps into his Eternal Destiny.

In <u>The Book of the Sacred Magic of Abramelin the Mage</u>, the supposed author Abraham offers a piece of advice which is rarely considered in modern occult practice: "Furthermore it is likewise necessary to think and consider whether your goods and revenue be sufficient for this matter; and, further, whether your quality or estate be subject unto others, ye may have time and convenience to undertake it." Abraham reiterates the point in the following two chapters by cautioning, "a valet, lackey, or other domestic servant, can with difficulty arrive at the end required, being bound unto others and not having the conveniences at disposal which are necessary, and which this Operation demandeth… Ye shall therefore seek retirement as far as possible; until that ye shall have received that Grace of the Lord that ye ask. But a Domestic Servant who is compelled to serve a Master cannot well have these conveniences (for working and performing the Operation.)"[1]

The author of the text, whether such is in actuality the figure identifying himself as Abraham the Jew or if it is instead some other more or less illustrious historical character writing under pseudonym, puts before the Aspirant this knowledge that may very well mean his success or defeat in the matters of Ascent. A gross percentage of those practicing the occult or following the lifestyle of either ancient or New Age religion find themselves at the lowest rung of the industrial latter for a good part of their lives. Often, it is their perpetual suffering in life that runs parallel to their interest in the occult, and it is ironically this inexorable draw that could end their suffering at any given moment. Nearly every time I have given to my students and to those who walk paths similar to mine the same advice as Abraham gave, a whining chorus sets in.

"I *can't* make more money right now; things are just too stressful as it is," "I *can't* find a job that will pay me more and allow me the freedom and time to do what I know is most important in my life; I've tried!" or, "It would take a miracle to make that kind of income and free up the majority of the day." All of these are wonderful excuses, but nothing more. You have summoned to physical materialization any spirit that you have desired. You have commanded that spirit to do your will, and it has. You command invisible armies, if you choose to. You work miracles in your life, if you choose to. You hold all of the power of God, if you choose to.

"Why such focus on filthy lucre, anyways? Isn't this *spiritual* Ascent that we're talking about."

Firstly - no! Ascent is the raising of the *whole* being to a state of limitlessness. It is difficult, if not impossible to fathom that a person who is capable of wielding omnipotence is not limited by the eight dollar an hour job serving fast food. It is difficult to imagine that bagging groceries or organizing videotapes is fulfilling in every way. These jobs are important, in some obscure way, to the continuance of a society that is perpetually spiraling downwards in their neon and florescent distractions from the real meaning of life. They are great for people – but *we* are not people. We are Gods in the making, omnipotent beings that are just learning to crawl in these bodies of flesh. *We* demand more!

Second, the object is not money, but is freedom. An interesting observation, especially in the culture of the United States, is that the less you are paid, the more is expected of you. If you left your job today, how long would it take your employer to replace you? If you wanted to take a month off to pursue your true interests, would you be paid for that time? If you desired more out of your job, your time, your days, and your life, could you get it? You most definitely could, if only you desired it badly enough to rise up again in the shadows of creation and give your command.

In 1943, Abraham Maslow published a paper entitled <u>A Theory of Human Motivation</u>[2], which proposed that as a person meets his or her most basic, survival needs, he or she will naturally be inclined to look towards the fulfillment of greater needs, the accomplishment of more widespread goals, and the realization of higher aspects of his or her self. This hierarchy is most often depicted in the form of a pyramid, the most instinctual needs of physiological health, the ability to eat and drink, sleeping, and basic hygiene at the base of the pyramid, and the greatest goals of self-actualization and spiritual ascent at the peak of it, all things in between acting as a type of personal and psychological latter that must be climbed a rung at a time, each step allowing the traveler to move his attention upwards.

Maslow's self actualization takes its greatest form in spiritual Ascent. Often, the whole of his pyramid is surpassed when the Sorcerer steps onto this path into Eternity. He no longer struggles to define himself or to find his place in the world, but instead discovers his place beyond this world, beyond the body of flesh and the meaty brain. His work is now to uncover his place within the Eternal, as well as the place of the Eternal within him. His goals reach beyond this life and deeper than this earth, and his every Operation builds not for today or tomorrow, but for all time.[3]

It is necessary before seeking to lift your Magickal throne above the stars of God to secure all of your base needs here on the dust of the earth. You hold in your hands at this moment the keys of knowledge that will unleash the power to raise you from a beggar to a king. Through evocation your finances will be made sure, a permanent place of residence can be secured, your body can be invigorated, your health will be fortified, your life can be lengthened, relationships can be strengthened, and in short, all waters of your life will be made aright.

Having put the knowledge and experiences gained in the first part of this book towards actual real world goals, and thereby having lifted your eyes from the dust and the dung of life and into the fiery whirlwind of possibility, you may open the doors to that palace which will grant you limitless power, knowledge, ability, and growth.

A spiritual mentor of mine once likened all of creation unto an intricate machine built by the Eternal creative force to expand, sustain, and eventually destroy itself, and to be rebuilt again. The purpose of this machine is to house God, or the Source of all things. As the voice and the light of the Eternal Source moved out into the void, creation expanded from the Source in concentric circles or ripples in nonexistence. The farther the ripples moved from the Source, the more solid they became, until finally creation made its last ripple as far away from God as it could get: manifesting as the physical plane. The natural inhabitants of these various planes, having been born into the Soul Planes, the mental plane, the astral, and so forth, were born into a state of real and inseparable attachment to that plane. While those in the realms and states of existence which remain nearer to the Eternal could view, act upon, and even enter into the planes below, those above are entirely inaccessible; therefore, the only thing that could travel upwards and inwards indefinitely is God itself.

In order to dwell in the lowest regions of creation, the darkest domain of existence, and to experience being removed from Its own grace, this omnipresent Source which created all things and is the power of the motion and stillness of all things then breathed Its own essence, Its force, power, knowledge, and prescience into creatures living in the machine. These animals in that instant began a process of transmutation, their bodies, minds, emotions, awareness, and abilities developing, naturally becoming over time like unto that Source which is the soul within. While every other creation in the physical universes, although they all possess the energy and vital force necessary to sustain themselves indefinitely in the physical plane, are not capable of directly gaining knowledge of the planes and states above, or learning the secrets of higher realms from the entities of those realms, these Divine creatures, human beings, being God incarnate, are.

The Eternal soul of man, being wrapped up in the attachments of his nature and choosing, remains bound to this plane only until It is capable of accepting at least a portion of Its True Identity, and from that instant the person, the flesh-and-blood human being, will continue his or her development, to no longer be bound to the flesh but to break free into everlasting power. As the God within is piece-by-piece let loose in the life of the man, that power will shine into the darkness of this lowest hell and all of creation will remember and will recognize its Master. The elements of the earth will obey him, blood will flow or will boil at his call, and celestial bodies will realign to answer to his will. And as he looks beyond this life and this plane, as he enters the other realms, and as he calls entities from those realms into this world, his Godhood will unfold even more, and those higher planes and all of their inhabitants will react as was evidenced in the physical plane, recognizing the power that has set them in their places.

In this whole machine of creation, the concepts of good and evil exist only within the mind of man. Throughout the remainder of existence, necessity dictates action. The Eternal Source does not question the morality of the thing when It breathes creation from Its bowels. It does not do a good deed when It provides the things necessary for Its creation to sustain itself, and It does not feel guilt when the whole thing is destroyed by blue flame and breathed back into Itself. Likewise, angels do not bow any lower before the immeasurable presence of the Eternal than demons, for their power is one in the same, and their purpose is identical, although their methods and natures differ. That basic function for which all things have been created is for the experience of the Absolute within the framework of the finite, expressed Eternally as a million souls that are tiny flames, combined to create a sea of fire.

While this explanation of the Ascendant Magician's ability to conjure, constrain, and command any entity whatsoever can and is dismissed entirely as gratuitous egocentrism, it does nevertheless inspire a look at and a moment of thought for the basic fact that the Sorcerer is indeed at the head of his empire and if he so chooses, the entire habitation of this reality machine will fall under his dominion. The introspect might also consider that the only reason a demon, angel, elemental, spirit, or even any of the so-called Gods would not bow to him faithfully is that he, the hopeful Aspirant, would not bow before himself were he able.

Supernal Servitors

Angelic choirs are automatically and almost immediately brought to mind when one imagines the types of entities that exist for the sole purpose of the uplifting of men and the spiritual progress of the Magician. While they serve the same Master as their demonic brothers, as well as every other type of entity, angels provide the most direct assistance in matters of self-knowledge and Ascent. The power held by angels is difficult to match, as is the speed at which they are able to accomplish whatever goal they agree to. The task in working with them, however, is that they must be convinced of your need for such intervention, and they are not easily lied to.

A majority of the Sephirotic angels are adept at perfecting specific aspects of the Evocator's life: manifesting amounts of money if needed, healing loved ones, helping with business matters, teaching certain arts and sciences, along with an entire plethora of powers which in themselves may not appear to be related to Ascent directly. An unfortunate assumption commonly made is that spiritual development and Ascent consists of rituals and ceremonies that have no practical use or application, but in some way lead to the supposed exaltation of the Magician. In actuality, every action is a step in Ascent, whether that action is the evocation of the burning Seraphim or skimming the latest tabloid articles. As human beings, imbued with the essence of Godhood, we are in a constant state of Ascent, always learning something about ourselves and our world, always becoming a more enhanced version of what we were yesterday. While binding states such as drug addiction, alcoholism, sexual mania, and politics are without a doubt of their own virtue negating to spirituality, when the addict is seen on the other side, she will always proclaim that through such states of psychological and spiritual imprisonment she came to learn more about herself than at any other time in her life.

With Magick, we are able to accomplish the greatest amount of work in the least amount of time by combining several natural forces and powers for one task. A mountain may crumble into dust over millennia, and another may rise over an equal amount of time, but when the Master motions towards it and commands with all of his will, "Remove hence to yonder place," it shall remove, "and nothing will be impossible unto you."[3] In the same manner, when the Sorcerer learns to manipulate and guide the forces governing the Lower Planes through the same ancient sciences, he sets into motion an unstoppable momentum towards Ascent, and this is never more directly evident than when working with angels. While they can lay thousands of dollars at your doorstep, sometimes within hours, you can be sure that the money will in some way end up doing some considerable good in your life or the lives of others. They touch the lives of those who call on them with such a Divine grace that the path the Evocator walks will light up with purpose and the abundance they receive will carry them higher into the heavens than any mortal would dare to fly.

The archangels, however, work much more directly on the unfolding of the Supersoul. If you are ill and summon Raphael, you will find that your body heals quickly, but also that emotional and psychological damage will begin to repair itself, and that even the elusive idea of your "spirit" will mend where it has been broken. You will Ascend by virtue of having called into this plane and into your life an archangel to work upon you. The archangels are thought to be the immediate intermediaries of the Will of God, Divine Providence being given directly to them, who then delegate it to the angels, who act upon the world of man to bring the Kingdom of Heaven to earth. While the archangels are also considered the ruling entities of the planetary spheres, or the Sephirah, by their nature they are not limited to those spheres or their supposed stations, but instead work towards the one goal of the Ascent of man, and to that end will do all that is necessary.

Given below is a list of angels and archangels that are to be evoked, in the given order. This will act as a pathworking, the Evocator traveling the path of Ascent one sure step at a time under the guidance of the angels. As the Sorcerer summons each of the angels, new doors of understanding, power, and ability will be opened. Through this simple process, if the guidance of the angels is accepted, the Evocator will find herself nearer to her own godhood than she would ever have imagined.

I.   Deggal is a glorious angel who appears as a figure so engulfed in Divine Light that his features are hidden in the brightness of it. Even his voice seems to come from this mantel of light rather than from his mouth, the illumination itself creating the pure sound of his voice. When Deggal materializes and is greeted, he is to be tasked to surround you with his light, which he likely will do in a gesture of his hands. When he so gestures, unless the angel instructs you in another method for receiving his mantel, it will appear as a bright blanket of light moving from his personage to yours. This light, although your conscious awareness of it will swiftly fade, quickens your energetic vibrations as well as all of the invisible vibrations in your immediate environment, setting the stages for Ascent within and around you. Deggal may also provide other instructions for strengthening this envelope of light, as well as giving you instructions for enhancing your own aural vibrations.

II.   Sakatos is a cleansing angel who materializes in the form of a strong young man riding in the center of a whirlwind. When he first appears, his arms are stretched out to his sides, his fingertips touching the swirling walls of the whirlwind around him, seeming to keep the whole of the thing balanced in motion. The whole power and might of this angel is focused upon clearing any obstacles from your path of Ascent and removing chaos from your life, and it is to this end that you will evoke him. When Sakatos has manifested before you, converse with him concerning the nature of any obstacles you might face in the near future pertaining to your spiritual and Magickal development. Take into serious consideration any advice that he might give, and discuss options for ridding your life of these obstacles as efficiently as possible. You then may charge him with the task of removing any of these obstacles, or others, from your path entirely. If you do give this command, however, be certain that the stumbling blocks in your way are ones that you can live without. Sometimes the prayer of, "God, teach me humility," invokes less mercy than, "God, I'll figure it out myself!"

III.   Raziel is a tall archangel who manifests with enormous blue wings and wears a gray robe that seems to be made of some sort of ethereal material that is constantly in motion. His presence is nearly suffocating, his ancient power drowning the Temple. Raziel is the keeper of the secrets of all of the power of God, the silent witness to the creation and destruction of all things, the One who knows the word by which the universe was created, and the word by which it may be brought to an end. Raziel is to be evoked no less than four times before moving on to Derdekea. In the first evocation, you will simply tell him that you wish for all of the secrets of Eternity to be revealed to you, in time. Ask for his advice on beginning this path of revelation, and if he gives any such advice, follow it closely. If he speaks but one word, know that that one word is the key to heaven. On the second evocation, give any necessary report concerning the exercises he has given you, and request that he surround you with servitors or familiars who will constantly guide you in discovering the hidden parts of yourself and your universe. On the third evocation, request that he himself puts into action occurrences, objects, or people that by their nature will directly reveal the next steps you are to take in Ascent. You are not to look for these changes in your environment, searching for something until it comes, for it will be undeniable once it is before you. On your final evocation, you are to ask the Archangel Raziel for a word. He will speak this word, or you may have a piece of parchment lain in the Triangle beforehand upon which he will write it, although rarely he will as the word he gives you can never be repeated or given to another. This word is to be brought to mind when considering the things of Eternity and questing for power, and the simple thought of it will realign galaxies to reveal the path.

Deggal

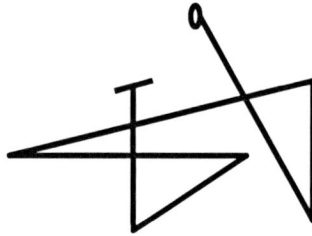

Sakatos

Raziel

Derdekea

Metatron

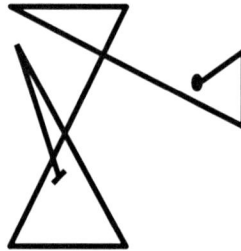

Enkidorat

IV.   Derdekea is the beautiful angel of mercy and salvation. She is the surrogate mother of all mankind, the angelic sister of the Saviors of this earth, the one fairest angel who can soften hearts of stone and lift the Sorcerer's eyes to meet the face of God. Her skin is porcelain and her robes are woven from the Love of God itself. Her eyes appear to always hold back tears as she takes on the sins of the most wicked men so that they may Ascend without the chains of guilt and negative attachment to the past. Often in the dark and secret works of Magick, the Sorcerer will find himself in a place beyond redemption by conventional means. Our True Identity shouts and urges that we are beyond good and evil and that we are not bound by the past, but that animal shell that we inhabit will not believe. We feel shame for the instincts that have allowed us to dominate while all other species have floundered, for our violence, greed, lust, and pride. Ironically, it is the guilt itself that keeps us from raising above the animal self into a realm of boundless purity. Whether we have slaughtered children or stolen candy, there is something in almost every person's life that does not sit well with them – especially in regards to those of us who keep both feet in hell, hands reaching towards heaven. Derdekea will relieve this all, will cradle you in her arms, and will pour the most Divine Love upon you, which is the only baptism that can wash away <u>our</u> sins.

V.   Metatron manifests as a tall man whose face is young and vibrant yet ancient and knowing at once. Brilliant light in every color of the spectrum radiates from the center of his being, illuminating the entire Temple. It is this angel whose softly spoken words can open the doors to Godhood. When evoked, he will give you simple exercises that will purge weakness from your being and will lift your understanding into the knowledge of Eternity. Once Metatron has been summoned, his influence will remain effective for the remainder of your existence. It is his light which will guide you on the Path of Ascent, and it is his influence which will place on that road all of the things that you will need for your eternal unfolding. After evoking Metatron, you will find opportunities arising quite spontaneously to unite with other people in learning, to gain membership in esoteric lodges that had once been hidden, and to be initiated, either through spiritual Masters or through your own efforts, into the secret understanding of everlasting Godhood.

VI.   Enkidorat materializes as a glorious angel in shining white robes and blond hair that flows behind him in the astral winds. He is extraordinarily large in size, and the spiritual greatness that radiates from him is overwhelming. When he speaks, his voice seems to come not from his lips, or even from the figure standing within the Triangle, but rather from above like rolling thunder. Call upon Enkidorat only when you have been prepared by the five preceding angels, and when he looks upon you he will invite you into the glory and power of Godhood, and will give you the tools and knowledge of the arts of creation and destruction, that you may act as God over an existence that has become yours.

Demonic Ascent

There is a power in darkness whose characteristics are entirely unique and irreproducible in any other form, which puts into the hands of the Sorcerer the ability to devastate lives, to shake nations, to call the earth into revolt and the stars into rebellion. While the potency of baneful Magick, blood ritual, and works of domination has been a constant pestilence to the inhabitants of the earth, there are few Works of Darkness more terrifying and more capable of turning raw desire into reality than demonic evocation. Demons will help the Evocator in Ascent, not by some vacuous sense of righteousness or godliness, but by the unbridled power to create and destroy, to effect undeniable change in the physical world. Demons do not question the morality of a thing, but like the Gods of every civilization they act upon this physical reality in a way that leaves no question of the source of the disease.

Magicians will summon demons to appearance before them, but will cling tightly to what they believe to be acceptable and safe while in the presence of embodied evil. These demonic Dabblers insist that such works are not wicked or sinister, but are merely "dark," which of course is simply a shade of "light." Here, we must delve into the forbidden to fully possess the cursed powers of the demons, to command the tides of destiny as they do, to take all that is desired as they do, to kill as they do, to live as Gods while trapped in hell. The modern Magician walks a silver thread of a line when dealing with demons, hoping that at the final dreaded moment he can jump back to safety on the light side of the fence. Here, we instead must leap into the pit itself, to be devoured in that Lake of Fire so that we may be reborn without fear, doubt, or limitation.

Demonic evocation is most commonly used to obtain something in life that is otherwise unattainable, and the demons are quick to respond and to deliver. Their greatest powers, however, lay hidden from the eyes of the average Evocator as they wait centuries for one to summon them and demand that which is forbidden. Although the use of demonic allies will be embedded into some of the most Ascendent rituals in the remainder of this text, it is in the evocations which immediately follow that the Evocator will divorce himself from his previous myths concerning evil and will experience the real thing.

While, like archangels, there are archfiends, Grand Demons, and devils in most every culture that are capable of giving godlike power to those who would dare call their names, the very nature of demons, regardless of rank, is to lust for power in its many forms. Most any demon can and will aide the Sorcerer in his personal quest for power, which by definition is the quest for Ascent, a search for one's own inherent godhood. If you ask them, they will work the impossible for you. If you demand it, however, they will show you how to do the same for yourself. Demons have discovered the secrets to manipulating the forces that sustain the three realms farthest from the Light of God. There exist methods and works by which the demons will teach the Evocator these very secrets, tutoring her in the ways that she might use the same power, giving her keys to demonic control.

Despite whatever relationship you have established with demons in previous evocations, this first demon you should summon on your pathway of demonic ascent is the Goetia's Belial. The demonic King Belial offers dignities, presidencies, offices, and general rulership over the earth and its intelligent powers. This demon extends another offering, however, which is not given in any book, nor is it readily discovered by the average Magician evoking Belial to help with job advancement or social intrusion. Belial is one of the four demonic gatekeepers to the doors of the inferno, which is the place not where the weak souls burn, but the refinery in which the weakness *within* soul is incinerated.[4] This fact will be refuted by most who have not worked with demons in general and Belial in particular in the matter of Ascent, citing that the Belial that is given in the <u>Goetia</u> is not the ancient rebellious devil, and that his powers are indeed limited to that which the author lists in the book, not giving thought to the possibility that the author may be limited to that which the demon has revealed to him, nor to the pre-Judaic existence of the entity. The devil takes many forms, each one suiting the respective Evocator's needs and desires…, and level of preparedness. Belial comes quickly when called, his presence storming the Temple like a smothering sandstorm. His essence is black and secretive, as he is one of the grand chiefs of the great secrets of demonic power.

The study of practical demonolatry has uncovered a strange oral phenomenon known as "demonic Enns." Enns, as the term was put into circulation by Alexander Willits in the mid 1500's, are short incantations given in an unidentifiable language which claims to call upon the power and presence of the demon for which the Enn is recited. Some modern, and historic, demonolaters even go as far as to claim that the Enns were given to Sorcerers by the demons themselves. Whatever the origin, the Enns as known today have appeared in at least a few journals and writings in exact concordance with one another, despite era and location. In the ritual of evocation for the materialization of Belial, the altar must face towards the north or the west. While gazing into the demon's sigil, rather than calling his name instead call the demonic Enn that has been associated with him: "Lirach Tasa Vefa Wehlc Belial," repeatedly as Belial materializes before you.

When he finally stands within the Triangle, greet him and issue the command, "Belial, throw open the gates of Godhood to me. Grant me entrance into the infernal kingdoms of Perdition. Lower me into Hell, and bring Hell to me. Take me into your palaces of flame and teach me the secret keys of power."

Belial's first reply to this request will ordinarily be that of a test. He may give you an exercise that has in itself no merit. Those that accept the task will wander from that point into an aimless eternity. If Belial offers a task, consider it carefully and weigh the value of it against all that you have learned from your experience in ritual, meditation, and evocation. If the demon senses fear or lack of confidence in any degree, he will use this as the first test, sometimes assuming terrible forms, speaking in a rough and threatening voice, assailing the senses of the Operator with visions of damnation, or playing upon the specific fears of the Evocator directly. To these tests, the only reply should be, "Belial, great demon of darkness, I have summoned you here before me so that I may lift my throne above that of God, and that in darkness I may Ascend. Grant me now the knowledge that I seek, and guide me towards my Destiny." While Magicians of a medieval bent feel that a statement such as this threatens the demon and "puts him in his place," those who work closely with them know that it is power only that demons respect, and that worship is reserved for the dead and dying.

Belial will then begin to converse with you concerning the exact powers that you wish to master, and the methods by which such Adepthood may be procured. From that moment, he will prepare the world around you for your Ascent, and when you leave the Temple you will feel his presence around you, often uncomfortably close to your skin, his influence guiding you, his power enveloping you, his blackness merging with your own energy.

Azazel has been a demonic Promethean figure throughout the history of religion, appearing in various texts as the revealer of the secrets of power, the demon who taught men to forge weapons and to wage war, the Watcher who gave mankind more knowledge and power than they could sustain, and have been wandering in confusion and spiritual pestilence ever since. Azazel is the demon who whispers the confidences of the Gods into the ears of men, who leads the multitudes into the sea with promises that they might learn to walk upon it. Azazel. Azazel. Even the speaking of his name brings him near.

Repeating his name as you draw him into the Temple and into the Triangle, lose yourself in the oral repetition. The necessary rapture will come much more quickly and much stronger in the evocation of Azazel, and as his presence distills into the Temple you will know that he is ancient and powerful without end. Several

111

spirits will move and dance around the Circle, the black angels of Azazel heralding his manifestation.

Azazel is always more than delighted to reveal the secrets of power once he stands before you on the Temple's ground. There is nothing that he cannot teach, if he is asked. The demon may also develop for you a regimen of meditations, exercises, and rituals that will increase your natural power and your ability to use that power. Azazel will attempt to push you farther and higher than you believe you are capable. He sees the god within all people, and struggles to bring that inner omnipotence to the surface.

The demon Aosoth, although not one of the "certified" demonic gatekeepers of Ascent in darkness, has nevertheless proven to be a powerful ally and instructor in achieving states of self godhood. Aosoth will take on a diversity of forms, appearing as a man, woman, an agendered personage, as a cumulative darkness, or even in the guise of the Evocator himself. When the demon speaks, its voice does not betray a gender, nor does its dialect give hint to any era or geographical place.

My own journal of metaphysical experimentations bears record of my evocation of Aosoth. The moment that the demon's sigil came to life upon the altar, its presence rushed

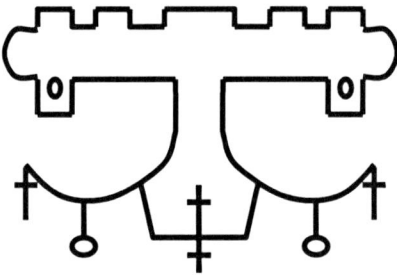

Belial

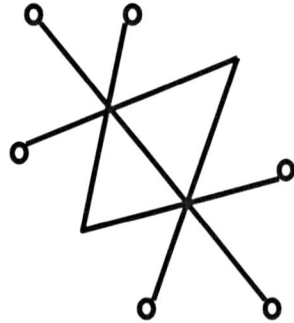

Azazel

into the room. I called the conjuration, drew the demon to the space before me, and its materialization was nearly instantaneous, although not altogether solid. Instead of a body, I saw in the air before me the whole of the universe, as if an ethereal projection screen was place there in the Triangle to show me all of creation in a flash. As the planets, comets, suns, and space flew by my vision, I saw that it suddenly ended at what is referred to as the Acausal Border, the event horizon of the abyss. Aosoth then materialized a body of shifting blackness and began to speak, becoming only the second time in my decades of evocation that an evoked entity has spoken before being greeted. The demon's greeting to me, the supposed Operator of the ritual, was brief, although very personal to my own progress at the time.

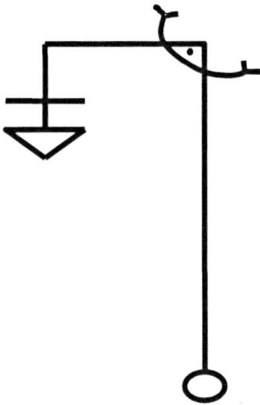

Aostoth   Adramelech

My first command to the demon Aosoth was to, "Surround me and impale me with power. Heighten my abilities and my Vision. Grand unto me all of the glory of the Dark Gods."

"In time, all shall be yours," Aosoth reassured. "Remember always to be vigilant. There are those that wish to overthrow you, even within your own. Destroy them with metal and fire. I will help you do this."

Within a week of this admonition, ranking members of the occult lodge in which I held similar status attempted to turn the head of the order against me, and succeeded. Shortly after, the whole order was disbanded, and the mutinous were left in the shark filled waters.

Aosoth advised me in methods of increasing the potency and efficacy of my spiritual vision, and even as I spoke with the demon I could feel that sight being pried open wider, could feel the rapture of the evocation pushing me beyond sanity, and could see farther and deeper than ever before. In my journal I recorded concerning the awakening of my vision even after the end of the evocation, "I can feel my vision and all of my senses heightening already. I'm staring into a whole different world; a world populated with nothing. It is the future unformed, the brink of creation, and I am the sole inhabitant. The future forms around me, from within. Every thought is an act of god."

Adramelech is the Lord Chancellor of Hell, and is said to preside over the High Council of demons, although such a title was surely invented by Christian demonologists to denote a societal structure in Hell similar to that on earth. Most sources ascribe animalistic features to the manifestations of Adramelech, often being said to manifest as a peacock or as a figure with the torso and head of a man with arms and legs of a mule. The only reason that Adramelech would initially materialize in this form is if such an image were expected by the Operator from the onset of the ritual. Otherwise, the demon will usually manifest in quite a human form, albeit a few feet taller than average with a muscular build – a veritable demonic juggernaut.

Being the Evil Chief of the Qlippothic Sphere of Samael, Adramelch will give you instructions for rituals that will alter your environment and events of the near future in a manner conducive to a union with what he refers to as your "Demon Self." He will also offer a structured pathworking of evocations of demons subordinate to him that will individually guide you in various aspects of your own dark alchemy.

Evoking the demons listed above and receiving the assistance that they offer in Ascent and mastery over demonic power is a direct and effective way to obtain that which you seek. The Evocator can still lower himself yet another level into Outer and Inner Darkness through the use of demonic pacts. For some, the mere evocation of demons is a long reach from that which was once comfortable and safe, and perhaps for others it is simply a necessary beginning to a long journey into darkness. Either way, however, as long as the Operator limits his experience with demons to the day and hour of evocation, he creates a definite distance between that Magickal, powerful part of his life and the everyday routine. His rituals yield success, the demons fly out into the world and bring it to his feet, yet he is able to compartmentalize these personae to the point that in the daytime he fails to fully appreciate the majesty of his Work. The demonic pact does not allow such forgetfulness.

In defense of demonic pacts, the demonist will often point out that traditional evocation attempts to coerce the demon into a situation wherein only the Magician is rewarded. The pact, then, assures that both parties are satisfied. This mentality reflects the two most major erroneous beliefs concerning demons and pacts with them. The first assumption made is that since the Evocator does not witness a direct exchange of services, the demon obviously receives nothing from helping him. The second assumption, which is borne of pure egoism, is that since the Magician did not personally give the demon something, the demon must have received nothing, because the Magician is the giver of all things, ignoring the fact that an ancient, intelligent, and powerful entity which has existed long before the first incarnation of the Sorcerer, happens to be standing in the same room, surrounded by the same air as the Operator.

If a hot, delicious meal is placed on the table before you, would you ask your host what she will give you for eating her food? When a lover offers her body and heart, do you question what you might get out of the task of making love? Just as the nature of man is to eat, to kill, and to procreate, and with social taboos removed he will do these to his heart's delight, the nature of the demon is dominion. Petty trinkets do not interest the demonic, nor do "special favors." Power and the exercise of that power are sublime.

The most common mythological demonic pact is the one in which the soul of the Operator is promised to the demon upon death if it delivers a set amount of goods and favors before that finality. Demons have no use for human souls. They own no crystal prisms in which to trap the promised spirits, nor are they greatly concerned with what becomes of the person's Eternal Being after death. Demons hunger for power, and as they have accrued unthinkable amounts of it through time and experience, they begin to thirst to use that power. They wait with baited breath for an Evocator to challenge them with a task for which they may have to assert some real effort and put into full effect the supernatural strength that they have acquired. A demon can materialize in a million forms in millions of Temples in the space of one night, instruct numerous Magicians in methods of gaining power and control over the lower worlds, and put into effect in the subtle planes an energy current which will gather momentum to eventually fulfill the requests of millions of Sorcerers, without straining any metaphysical muscles. The demon has gathered unimaginable power through time, and has refined its ability to use that power in a real and tangible way. It now waits to be called and to be given a task that requires planning, constant attention, and forceful will. The sole exhilaration of the demon is the exercise of its power, the utilization of its full potential. Humans are not so different.

A true pact with a demon, or any other entity, is not necessarily one in which the demon agrees to do something for the Evocator, and in return the Evocator will do something else for the demon, but is instead when the Sorcerer and the demon work together, uniting to accomplish a single goal. Having used evocation and ritual to gain the things of this earth all that is left is to move beyond the flesh into the realms of godhood. The demon recognizes this as Ascension to the state of absolute domination of existence, and will always oblige. One of the most potent pacts the Sorcerer can make with the demon towards this end is for the ability to call on the demon's aid, his familiars, or his power without having to perform a full evocation. Once such a pact is made, all that is necessary is for the Sorcerer to enter a state wherein his will and power may flow, such as can be attained through simple meditations, and to call the name of the demon with whom the pact was made or to call a "word of power" given to him by that demon. Almost immediately the Sorcerer will feel the presence of the demon enter the room, not in a condensed embodiment as would present itself in evocation, but a liquid essence that gathers around the Caller and waits to be commanded. Gain a clear mental image of the effect for which you are Working, release the fear and doubt that normally impedes success, sense with certainty the demonic powers and entities around you, and state your command in as simple and blunt terms as possible. Being of a more traditional slant, I prefer to begin the command as, "In the name of, demon's name, I command..." or "By the power of demon's name, I command..."

It is always a good idea to set a timescale for this type of assistance, rather than allowing an unstoppable force to invade your life for an indefinite amount of time. You will notice that the longer the duration of this pact, the more spontaneous its effects become. One of my first students had a particular knack for evocation, and for sensing and communicating with entities at any time. He made the pact suggested above with a rather powerful and ancient demon, who immediately attached three familiar spirits or servitors to him. Within days he came to me for help in ridding himself of them. At all times he could sense them circling around him, and if he found himself daydreaming about something, reality would react as if his very thoughts could alter the physical world, as if there were no separation between thought and action. Set a reasonable amount of time with the demon when the pact is made, and when the term of the pact is over, summon the demon once more to thank it and to release both parties from its bonds.

A less agreeable form of Ascent through pure demonolatry is for the Sorcerer to submit himself to the will of the demon. These can often be the most terrifying pacts to make, to do that which the demon would have you do. Outside of perfect possession, turning your will over to the demons in the form of conscious obedience brings the Sorcerer closer to absolute Darkness and true evil than anything else he could ever experience. The demon will usually begin with simple tasks, small sacrifices to demonstrate the obedience of the servant. Once the disciple has performed two or three minor tasks, the demon will begin to rearrange his life until it is suitable for hell. Not surprisingly, Evocators utilizing this type of demonic communion are often led into criminal acts. With enough instruction, however, the demons will also guide him through such acts without every being discovered by authorities. Some Sorcerers are quick to summon a demon and ask it what it wishes for him to do, crossing fingers and praying hard that the demon will have him fulfill the depraved desires that he fears doing of his own accord. The Ascendant Magician, however, will usually find that rather than catering to his lusts and desires, the demon challenges him to do things which he never thought he could do, to live his life in a new way, if only just for days or weeks. The demon will command its new disciple to experience hidden aspects of himself, to realize that within his True Identity there is no separation, that at will he may become anything that he chooses.

Again, a specific duration should be established beforehand, and should be held to. While the demon will release you from bondage whenever you will it so, you may not be so willing to leave. There is an addiction in evil stronger than any drug, and it should only be yielded to under certainly controlled circumstances. Many who are already on sanity's border will be pushed to the point of never regaining their own will. The demons will most definitely exploit this, and live vicariously through their new host, either through continued commands or through full possession.

Lords of this World

Ascent will often take unexpected forms and manifestations, lifting the Sorcerer into the realms of Godhood when he is putting all of his energy and will into building a Kingdom of attachments, materiality, and power over this world. It is as if his True Identity and his pure will leads him in the path that he must walk, by the very steps that would normally guide a man back into the dust only to return here again in the body of an animal rather than a God.

The Sorcerer becomes God not by a single Messianic act or a few years of miraculous grandstanding, but rather through mastery of himself and of existence, one step at a time. Being in this world, he must therefore be lord of this world. The early alchemists recognized four base elements upon which all things were created and sustained: fire, water, earth, and air. Peering into the metaphysics and religions of the past we discover legions of entities whose creation and existence is devoted entirely to one of these elements – armies of spiritual soldiers each empowered to uphold a specific aspect of their element, each of the four camps led by separate Warlords who have power over the element in its totality.

These four elemental warlords, or as they are more commonly called, the Elemental Kings, listed below, are to be evoked within a Triangle outlined by their element, while the Evocator stands within a Circle of the same. For the evocation of Paralda, the Elemental King of air, simply draw the Circle and Triangle on the ground in colors of white or blue, or you may place burning incense around the circumference of the Circle.

As you evoke each of the four Kings, they are to be tasked to teach you mastery over their specific elements. To this end they will give you rituals, which will increase the elemental power within yourself, and exercises that will teach you to control the elements in the outside physical world. Work with one King only until you and he have decided that your training is complete, and move on to the next, until you truly are the Master of this world.

I. Djin is known to be the Elemental King of fire. He appears as a large, muscular man with flowing hair that appears to be made of fire itself. Djin will first teach you to master the element of fire within yourself, using such to raise your temperature, to strengthen your muscles, and to create explosive amounts of energy. He will then instruct you in the Operation of rituals of fire, using the pure astral element to encapsulate your will and bring it into manifestation. The first of these rituals will be performed while he stands instructing, after which you will be able to do them as needed at any time. He will give you guided meditations that will have the same effect and will allow you to influence fiery energies within and around you in seconds. Finally, Djin will teach you to manipulate the physical manifestation of fire.

II. Paralda is the Elemental King of air. He appears in various manifestations, sometimes as an armored knight and other times as a translucent embodiment of air. While Paralda can teach you to control the physical element of air in amazing and sometimes cataclysmic extremes, his true joy is to instruct his Magickal students in the arts of divination, clairvoyance, and astral projection, as well as the more mundane, and perhaps the more practical methods of attaining mental clarity, raising alertness and general awareness, and improving memory, often to a photographic degree if his instructions are held to.

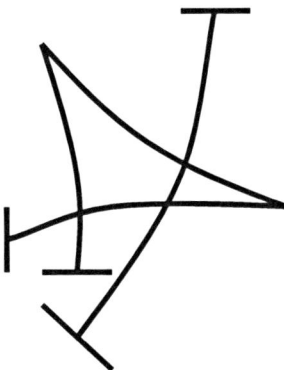

Djinn

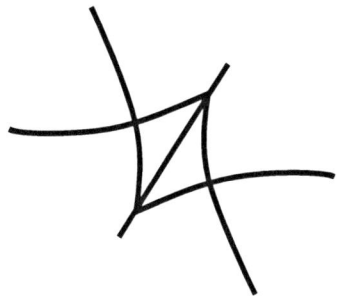

Paralda

III. Nachash is the Elemental King of water. He is young and beautiful with fair skin and kind eyes. Nichsah will provide a series of instructions that will first teach you to silently communicate with the elemental water within yourself and in your environment, which will lead to an inner understanding of influencing your life and the world through this inner connection. Nichsah will guide you into full control over fog, rain, and other manifestations of water, as well as the invisible realities of intuition, emotion, and relationships.

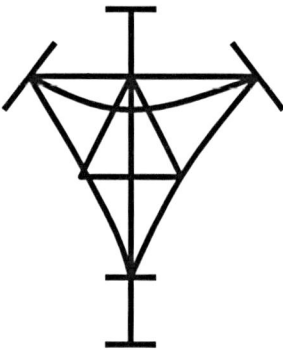

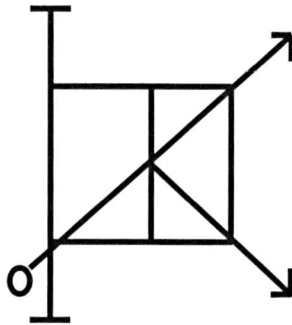

Nichsah   Ghob

IV. Ghob is the Elemental King of earth. Although he is often described as a generically Tolkien dwarf, Ghob just as often appears as a tall African man or as a fur and skin clad mountaineer. Mastery over the element of earth, especially when paired with fire, water, or wind can allow the Sorcerer to create or quell tornados, earthquakes, volcanic eruptions, and several other calamities. Studying the element and its powers under Ghob will also allow the Evocator to cause the earth to deliver up its treasure and bounty. Everything from gardening to investing can be learned as an art and an understanding rather than a struggle when working with Ghob.

The Operator is constrained only by his own Will and the precepts of his personal destiny. Ascent in darkness or in light, by the planets or by the elements of the earth, in the name of God or by the power of one's own name – Ascent is still being had. The Sorcerer or Sorceress is nonetheless experiencing the heights of power and the depths of understanding. The Sephirotic Spheres can be traveled, their Archangels evoked one at a time, across the abyss and into the Heart of the Eternal. The devils can be summoned forth to give the secrets of their power and to open up the gates of hell and the door of the bottomless pit to those who ask with pure lust. The angels can be called upon, and they will attend and will offer the highest palaces of the Kingdom of Heaven. The Evocator will learn through those whose company he holds that he himself is powerful without end, capable without limit, and knowledgeable without bounds.

E.A. Koetting

Chapter Seven
Multiple Evocators

This world's first great civilizations, literally sprung up from nothing in earth's most desert and forsaken places, were sustained wholly by that which is now called Sorcery. Ziggurats and pyramids were built in exact locations to such perfect specifications that our greatest modern architects are baffled, to serve as a gateway into other worlds and realms. Temples were erected throughout the Mesopotamian region after the various solar and planetary gods, so that the devotees of the Deities would have places wherein they might walk and talk with their idols. In the initial phases of the development of human civilization, there existed a freedom of being and of doing that is only now trying to reemerge after centuries of suffocation, but is taking the form of a withered old woman begging for release. In the time of pure existence, when survival was so dire that no church had time for crusades and saviors took the incarnations of warlords, the greatest Works of Magick were not performed in hidden cellars or remote wooded clearings, but in Temples laden with precious metal and draped in the finest cloths. Ritual was not a sight of a young woman crouched over a single candle chanting rhyming incantations, but of several Sorcerers gathered in a circle, raising pure power around and within them, and raising the most fearsome entities before them. The witches and wizards of ancient times were the holders of the destiny of empires and the maker of the fates of war. Together they evoked devils and spirits and even gods to full materialization within their Temples, and together they wrote what has become the history of the world.

Evocation as a solitary practice is now considered to be the standard rather than the exception. Only when a Magician believes that he is not capable of viewing or in any way communicating directly with that which he evokes will he request the aid of another who claims to possess such abilities, the Operations resulting from the duo often becoming more a folie `a deux[1] than a mutual symbiosis. The famous case of this phenomenon is that of the well respected and recognized Dr. John Dee, whose life's great Work was to converse with the angels and discover their language, accompanied by the often despised and imprisoned swindler and falsifier, Edward Kelley, who saw the visions of the angels in their seer's stone and heard the angelic voices calling out in the Enochian tongue. Dee contracted the assistance of Kelley not because he couldn't see the angels himself, but simply because he had not *learned* to see and to hear them. He had no background or foundation of occult discipline outside of theory and postulation, and so his entire career rested on the proclaimed abilities of one man for his ability to behold things of another world.

It has been considered traditional from the first millennium A.D. until the past hundred years for the Evocator to bring into the Temple and Circle an assistant, usually either a priest, a child, or a young man, who will see to the necessitous operations of the Great Operation, such as keeping the brazier filled with incense and producing the implements needed for the ritual at the appropriate times. Even such an assistant, however, was not included in the ritual itself outside of these mundane procedures. In both cases given above, despite the number of bodies within the Circle during evocation, only one person performs the ritual itself.

The power of evocation and the solidity of the phenomenal materialization of the spirit is magnified and multiplied by the number of Evocators pouring their will into the ether and opening a gateway through which the ethereal may enter this world. Gathering a group of people who think it might be fun to try to summon a demon will at best produce no result, and at worst will produce negative results. The unprepared human psyche is not capable of withstanding the sensory assaults naturally produced by the evocation of certain entities, nor is the Dabbler equipped to defend against any spiritual warfare that may ensue. Most often, the Dabbler will see nothing, will hear nothing, and will experience nothing, and will either fabricate a feeling of "something there," or will confess that the whole ritual was a farce and that Magick and demons are equally insubstantial. Every so often, however, when the names of demons are called, the demons themselves will answer, and although they will not materialize in a beholdable form before the unprepared Evocator, the demons will nevertheless manifest in the would-be Sorcerer's life in a manner that can only be described as evil.

The priests and wizards who would summon the most ancient spirits into their Temples often spent the majority of their lives in strict devotion to the study of these forbidden arts, being brought up as children under the canopy of the esoteric sciences. They did not happen upon their godlike powers through reading a book or two and performing some "spell" or another, but through a life of sacrifice and dedication, the likes of which foster a certain knowledge of limitless possibility that in itself is capable of not only moving mountains, but of moving worlds. If you have been Working or even simply associating with occultists whose knowledge you respect and whose abilities you admire, these might be the first for you to consider involving in rituals of evocation. If your occult life has been a solitary one, perhaps evocation itself will provide an answer. With the power that you hold and that you put into play in your life, you can easily summon a ritual partner of your exact specifications to literally show up on your doorstep.

Another option for finding others with whom you may ritualize is to gain membership in a group set up for that exact purpose. While most occult lodges and esoteric orders exist for the ego-glorification of one or a few individuals, rather than for the Ascent of each willing and devoted member, they serve for a good forum in which to meet others, who most likely have become bored with the drivel and are looking for the next step to the next level. Such a step is the one that you are attempting to make, and which you are willing to include them in. I have often been accused of "infiltrating" religious and occult organizations with anything but pure intentions, and drawing out those who would otherwise continue to participate in group ritual, pay the annual dues, and above all, stroke the fragile confidence of the head of the order. Regardless of the destruction caused to the lower worlds and all of their institutions, man *must* Ascend.

Once a suitable group is assembled, which should initially consist of four persons including yourself, you can mutually decide whether or not you will confine the relationship to ritual. While having friends with whom you have experienced some of the most breathtaking phenomenon and ritual results is rewarding on its own, the actual Magick raised and the power produced from meeting with complete strangers at a pre-designated place and time and each powering their individual will into the ritual is difficult to overshadow with any amount of social acceptance. The conscious mind and all of its prejudices are removed. As you get to know your Working partners, you also begin to see their inherent human weaknesses. You see them as people as frail as you, if not more so. You trust them with your secrets, but you are unable to trust your life in the hands of their strength and their power. In ritual, all men become God, if only for a moment, but that is not the figure you see under the black hood because you believe that you know them, when all that you really know is the husk and its fleeting attachments.

The first Working that you are to perform is a simple group scrying project that will serve to align your senses and greater perceptions with one another. It will also allow each member to "feel out" the others as far as Magickal ability and raw spiritual power, which will certainly be sensed in this Operation.

For this attuning exercise, as well as for future group Operations, you will need to obtain or manufacture a scrying device. Many modern Magicians are using scrying mirrors in spirit communication and evocation, which are simple pieces of round, flat glass painted black on one side. For group use, a scrying mirror with a three foot diameter can be set flat atop a raised altar or a table, and gazed into by the standing Operators. Polished obsidian or granite can serve the same purpose. Naturally reflective surfaces seem to "work" more easily, however, with less coaxing from the interpretative mind and senses. A large steel or silver bowl can be adapted as a "cauldron," or even makeshift items like a large non-ornate garden birdfeeder or a serving bowl can be painted black and filled with water in which the senses can enter other dimensions of thought. Water is one of the most receptive and "conductive" physical constructs when used in ritual, and can easily become a gateway between the flesh and the Power. Once the Operator learns to gaze into its surface and allow her sight to travel infinitely until it reaches a specified destination, the medium of water can be used at any time for this type of extended vision. I have found myself staring into a glass of water at a restaurant table and viewing the secrets of my evening companion quite spontaneously. I have also held close acquaintance with a Sorcerer who would scry into a bucket of dirty engine oil, and claims that it is the best medium he has ever used!

Once your group has decided on and procured your scrying medium, assemble inside of the Temple, at a dark hour. Set the scrying device in the center of the Temple at the appropriate height. Ideally, the group should be standing, looking down into the portal, which would sit flat at about waist-level; if sitting is required or preferred, however, the portal can be set upon flat ground. A good deal of "seasoned" occultists will instruct the attentive audience to set the scrying device at a specific angle thought to allow perfect sight into the reflective surface without catching any of the Temple's three-dimensional objects in its glare. I have yet to find this advantageous in operational Magick, the logical mind taking the forefront, considering the possibility of incorrect angles not allowing the sight to open, or the fear of seeing objects in the mirror, which are thought to be spiritual, but which might possibly turn out to be physical instead.

The logical brain and the optical sight overwhelms the creative mind and the true Vision, and the Greater Power becomes incapable of accessing the realms and states of limitless possibility. When the scrying device is laid flat, parallel to the ground, it may very well catch images of stalagmites, clouds, stars, or ceiling fans that hang over the Temple. When the portal fills with white mist and the sight begins to travel through it towards the object, the physical world and all of is inane distractions melt, leaving the group of scrying Sorcerers lofty inhabitants of a vacant and perfectly receptive universe. Often occultism takes the form of a science which attempts to complicate that which is most simple, and often most atavistically, instinctually natural to the born Magician.

Gather around the scrying device or portal, each congregant standing at even intervals from each other. Hold out your right hands over the portal so that your palms hover off of the surface of the water or glass one or two inches. Bring your breath under your control, inhaling long and deep and letting the air out slowly. As your pranayama leads your mind and energies towards perfection, you will notice a definite magnetism between the palm of your hand and the scrying surface. The moment that you become consciously aware of this magnetic force, focus your mind entirely upon it. Take note of the sensation of the simultaneous attraction and repulsion, your hand being pushed away from the surface of the portal yet at the same time drawn back into it strongly enough that your hand will not escape from the tractor. Become aware as well that as you focus your attention upon this invisible force, that it spontaneously strengthens. The magnetism will increase, pushing your hand a noticeable amount higher than before, at the same time strengthening the downward pull, locking your hand into the new position until a higher one is found. When this entire process seems to have stabilized, your hand remaining in one position without much fluctuation aside from the normal ebb and flow of energy between your skin and the portal, quietly say the word, "ready," so that your comrades can hear. Continue holding your hand over the portal, allowing the magnetism to keep it in place rather than your muscle.

When each member has given the verbal signal that they are ready for the next stage of the Operation, lower your hands to your sides. This first step attunes your physical body and senses to the invisible forces that you will be uncovering through scrying. If your body can feel it, then you eyes can see it and your ears can hear it. You are a whole being, not a collection of random parts.

Look into the scrying device with a relaxed gaze, as if you are looking for a nearing person through a heavy downfall of snow, waiting for the figure to come close enough that you can see. Let go of your mind and release it from all expectation. Feel your vision being pulled into the portal. The closer that you come to full entry, to having your sight and your senses immersed in the other worlds through this medium, the more your lower self will resist. Your mind will begin to chide you, telling you that you cannot do this thing, that you are making a fool of yourself in front of these other people, or that *if* you mistakenly do see something, it will have been created by your own imagination, not by some real spiritual occurrence. Your physical body will also fight the experience, your muscles tightening, and your lungs not taking in air. Consciously regain command over your body and breathe deeply, allowing the air to bring your muscles into relaxation. Maintaining your easy gaze into the scrying surface, establish a breathing pattern of long breaths with short holds in between. As you are in the process of establishing this pattern, your vision will awaken even more. Often it is at this point that the scrying medium becomes foggy, a white mist filling the portal. This phenomenon can initially be discarded as a glare on the glass or a temporary visual impairment, the mist being excused away by an imaginary light source casting a faint reflection or the eyes watering and blurring the vision. The strange mist or fogginess that comes into sight, however, is a universal sign and marker of the scrying senses awakening, and is a definite precursor to full immersion in the vision.

Remaining steady in your silent will and your fixed receptive focus, the mist will clear and your vision will be entirely activated. It is largely disputed as to whether or not the physical eyes actually see the image that materializes in the scrying medium, and it is this question which dissuades a good deal of aspiring Seers from accessing their greatest abilities of perception. When the mist clears from the surface of the mirror, your mind will be drawn from this plane into another through the portal. Often, this will feel as if you are losing consciousness, in a manner that is very much the same as that experienced during evocation when the omnipotence flowing through you and the presence filling the room cause a type of rapture. As your mind is drawn into the blackness lying beneath the scrying surface, you will stand wavering between consciousness and unconsciousness, and will literally stand in the space between two worlds. In the quiet darkness of nonexistence, the vision will arise.

At this point, each Operator will have a unique and personal experience of the same vision. While the same spirit may sit on the other side of the psychic window, the brains of each Seer will interpret the sight differently. Although some may see inside of the glass or the water a vision dancing before them, others may have a similar image enter their minds and their inner vision. I have known those who, once their scrying vision opens, will obtain automatic imaginary impressions of the spirit that she is calling out to, but will hear a booming voice around her, as real to her as if the spirit were using a surround-sound speaker system in her Temple to communicate with her. One Magician might see, with his physical eyes, the spirit's face forming on the reflective surface of the portal, while the Sorcerer next to him will see the spirit's features spontaneously arise in his mind and might hold an entire conversation in his inner world. Both have seen the same vision, but it has manifested differently depending on the abilities and expectations of the Operator.

Often, if no ritual summonings, invocations, or other Magickal preparations have taken place, the visions received will be meaningless, or at the very best, random. Do not allow them to sway you one way or another, and do not allow them to discourage you, feeling as if because you are seeing nothing of value, you must have "done it" wrong. You have scryed into nothing, and you are receiving nothing. You have, up to this point, prepared yourself to See and to receive. Lock yourself into the psychological and spiritual state in which you are receptive to whatever visions may come, keeping control of your breath and allowing yourself to sink deeper into the inner silence and outer dimensions rather than rising back into the dying world of physicality. Once you have penetrated the white mist in the scrying medium, have divided your consciousness between this plane and the others beyond, and are ready to receive the visions that you will invoke, say the word, "In."

Your tone will likely be mellow in your trance state, and although the others need to hear you, your voice should not be forced louder, lest it disrupt the state that you have induced within yourself, and towards which the others are working. The speaking of this word acts as a signal to the others that you are ready to receive the visions that may come. Remember that you are not performing ritual to impress others or to prove your personal worth, but to have a real and verifiable effect on yourself, your life, your world, and existence as a whole. If every other Practitioner has given the signal that they are "in" aside from you, don't rush to give the final signal until you are indeed ready, or the whole group will be dragged into inefficacy, not only in this ritual, but in all others performed together. The other congregants, in the meditative and receptive state induced by scrying, will rarely be bothered by remaining in bliss for a few extra moments while you prepare yourself for power and ability beyond that which has ever previously been known.

Once each participant has reached the necessary stage of receptive spiritual alertness, in the same non-disrupting tone as before, still gazing into the mirror, and in vocal unison the group is to give the following incantation, having been locked into memory beforehand.

Itz ranta taz kallu taz tafta saz fallu
Sitz falta ihr talma sitz kaltu fen tazu
Vaskalla sen kira sen fanta it allu
Int itzu ihr fallu ihr kallu int ratzu

Empowered by the above incantation, vision flowing through the portal, call for the first vision: "Show us the mountainous landscapes of Hildal." The vision will materialize in the mirror, or the scrying surface will act as a nexion for the imaginative mind to interpret the vision; in whatever individual manner you are able to see, you will see. It is a common thing for a would-be Seer to accept the reality of the image before it has fully materialized, in much the same way the fledgling Evocator might begin commanding a spirit before it has actually taken form, simply because she has become aware of its presence. Relax your mind, release your expectations and your doubts, and allow the vision to form. The valleys and the peaks of the mountainous range will come into view, the thick, green life budding over it, creatures bounding over the rocks and behind the trees. *See* the image rather than simply viewing it. Once the mountain range has clearly formed in your Vision, in the same tone as before, state to your associates: "There." When all have replied in like, lift your eyes from the scrying surface to see each other. This will break the connection between your Sight and that place which you were seeing, clearing the psychological slate for the next vision.

The group then holds their right hands an inch or two above the scrying surface, as was done initially, and as soon as the Magickal magnetism is felt, each person moves their hand in small, clockwise circles, sensing the magnetic energy dragging with the movement, stirring the cauldron of black vision, preparing the portal for another projection. Gazing into the scrying device once more, your vision will reactive more quickly than before, the white mist will appear, and the portal will be ready to receive its command. All congregants' state: "Show us the secret island of Sabul." The scrying surface will usually first fill with an image of the ocean, and in that water the island will materialize. Allow your vision to sweep down onto its beaches and into its forests. When you can clearly see the island, say, "There." Again, when all of the others have responded, look up at one another, away from the scrying portal, and separate your minds from the island. Wave your hands over the surface of it again, and then return your vision to the device.

Call out together, "Show us the face of the demon Rhyae." This scrying experience is entirely unique, because while this specific demon is fully aware of your spying eyes, and therefore may interact with you unlike most other scrying subjects, it is not being evoked to the point of holding full conversation, and especially will not acquiesce to any requests or demands. When the face of the demon is seen, give the verbal signal of, "There," and maintain focus simply on the vision, putting forth strict discipline to not hold any sort of telepathic communication with it, as the demon will certainly attempt to engage in some sort of witty exchange.

When all have arrived at the vision of the demon's face, clear the mirror as before, and immediately drape it in black cloth.

The three visions given above have been used extensively as test-sites or targets to be scried into, remote viewed, or traveled to in astral travel, Soul Journey, and bilocation. The first two exist as actual places, although the names given to them are internal designators rather than that which might appear on any map. As these places are traveled to with more frequency, they will be found to host two of the most marvelous and potent Temples still in daily use on this planet. This is, of course, discovered only as a spiritual familiarity between the observer and the observed is created. The third vision, that of the demon Rhyae, has arisen through time rather mysteriously. The demon's very presence has assisted the development of the greater senses quite automatically, and while his name and sigil have not appeared in any grimoire or text to my knowledge, he is easily and graciously evoked when the Evocator is able to receive a sigil from him through the above scrying method.

After having obtained all three visions as a group, and having cleared and covered the scrying device, it may be desirable to put away all ritual items and leave the Temple for a more common place where the events of the previous hour or so may be discussed. I've always preferred twenty-four hour coffee houses for these post-ritual conferences. What's important after this first group Working is not that each person's vision is exactly identical to those of the other members. In actuality, it is the unique perspective that each person brings to the ritual, both in assertion and reception of power and will, which creates such a formidable alliance. What you are looking for, however, is that each person did indeed have their own experience and vision… that each one is able to recount something about it as if recounting a high school dance or first kiss, rather than regurgitating the expected answers. This is the most personal and intimate art, the union of Souls in Ascension towards Godhood, and there is no room for passengers.

This first group Working will automatically begin to align the vision and the senses of the participants, will cast aside the chaff, if

E.A. Koetting

any, and will form a spiritual bond that is not easily broken. Usually, within days of having performed the above, each of you will grow itchingly more anxious to meet again and to fly even higher into the night sky.

Group Evocation 1

The first evocation that will be performed as a group is the summoning of one entity by the simultaneous will and direction of each member of the group. The potency of group ritual in itself lies in the exponential power of each participant reacting upon the cumulative energies and will of the others to bring about one single goal. This is never more immediately evident than in evocation.

The Temple is to be prepared as usual, with the Triangle in the South. A mixture of sandalwood incense and Dittany of Crete is to be used for the incense of materialization. The spirit to be called is Abartala. The Circle, which is to be constructed as a mote filled with water for this evocation, should span a nine-foot diameter. The four congregants or Evocators will need to discuss and arrange the speaking order; the orations given in this ritual are divided into four parts to suit the present quartet of Sorcerers. An altar should also be set up, in the center of the Circle, at an approximate waist-height. Abartala's sigil should be drawn and placed face down in the center of the altar. At the four corners of the altar four blue candles should burn. The chalice should be set to the east edge of the altar, and should be filled with mead or sweet wine, and the dagger should be set in the west.

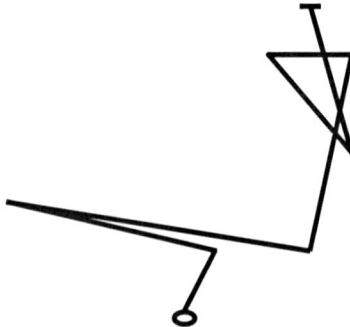

132

Gather around the altar, each member taking a perfect cardinal position, and invoke omnipotence as given in Chapter Three. Nearly every time that I have aligned with other Magicians for purposes of multiple group evocations over any considerable amount of time, I am amazed at how naturally the elemental roles and coordinating cardinal positions occur. I have yet to witness a squabble over which Evocator gets to stand in the south, and thus "represent" the element of fire, or over which Sorceress is most like the element of air. In planning and preparation for the first group evocation, I've noticed that we all seem to take our places quite naturally, and that as the ritual commences, it is vindicated that no other position would do as well for each particular Operator.

The initial preparations and consecrations should be observed, perhaps having one person consecrate the Circle, another, the Triangle, another, the altar, and the last to consecrate the ritual tools. Another method of group consecration would be to have each person consecrate each object, one after another, thus having all ritual devices consecrated four times, each member having put their own personal energy into the consecration. The latter option, of course, requires a great deal more time and coordination, but is well worth experimenting with.

When you have consecrated each of the necessary items, return to your places at the altar and flip the sigil so that it faces upwards, to be seen by the group. Each Evocator is to place his right hand on the altar, just below and to the right of the sigil. Gaze into the sigil briefly, until it begins to flash and your sight awakens into it, at which point you will quietly say, "In."

When the same signal has been repeated by all, call out in unison: "Abartala, hear our voices, see our signs, and know that we command the universe to bring you before us, so that we may see you, so that we may hear you, and so that your power will be our power, your strength will be our strength, and your knowledge will be our knowledge."

With the index and middle fingers, each Operator touches the face of the sigil and begins transferring the Divine Light, which is within into the parchment. Again in unison, state, "We seal this calling upon you, and we seal the power to perform this feat within this Temple in which you will manifest."

The Evocator standing on the southern side of the altar takes the chalice in his hands and holds it over his head, the base of the cup at third-eye-level, and calls, "I drink the blood of God. I take within me all of Its power." Drink some of the wine within the chalice, feeling the energy that has been infused in the fluid through the consecration refreshing the omnipotence within you, reawakening your senses and bringing your whole being back to life. He then replaces the chalice and the congregant to his left takes it in hand and does the same, until all four Evocators have partaken of the wine, consecrated as Divine Blood. Before moving forward with the ritual, a moment of silent observation should be observed, in which the participants may sense their own power permeating the Circle, as well as the attention and proximity of the spirit Abartala. As your senses attune to these things, signal your readiness to move forward by saying, "It is near."

When all four congregants have given the same signal, the Operator in the south pours a good deal of incense onto the burning coals in the brazier, filling the Triangle with smoke. The materialization of the spirit is at hand.

Replace your right hands on the altar and gaze again at the sigil. Allow your vision to open fully to see the essence of the symbol beneath the ink and paper. Breathe in deeply and sense the spirit coming near. Breathe out and see the lines of the sigil beginning to glow with power. When the entire sigil has transformed from something physical into a spiritual nexus centering the Temple in the metaphysical universe, signal this by saying, "Come."

When all have signaled likewise, and the presence of the spirit is sensed in the Temple, the participants remain standing in their places and face the Triangle. A united receptivity and activity begins here in which each member senses the spirit within the Temple, not as some vacuous force, but as an embodied entity who is only seconds away from assuming full physical form. As in the group scrying exercise, each Evocator opens his vision completely, the Triangle itself, and the smoke that fills it replacing the scrying mirror. As the sight and senses of the group attunes to the manifestation of the spirit, such manifestation will grow stronger, the force and presence of the spirit culminating critical mass, the spiritual and psychological rapture overwhelming the group. In the same manner as in individual evocation, the essence of the spirit will seem to move about the room at first rather than immediately gravitating towards the Triangle. Through the foggy blanket of rapture and the omnipotent force that overwhelms the flesh and the

Evoking Eternity

brain, the collective will of the group guides the spirit towards the Triangle, and at the same time pulls it through veils and planes towards the physical world, towards the Temple, into the Triangle. Incense is heaped upon the coals as needed, and that smoke will begin to solidify, to take on fleetingly physical shapes, heralding the emergence of the spirit into this world.

The Evocator at the south begins the conjuration: "Abartala, we call you and we conjure you forth to stand in this Temple and to take your place within the Triangle. We summon you to manifest before us in beholdable form and to speak to us in a discernable voice. Abartala, we give you license to appear, we give you power to manifest, we give you this call to come. Abartala, come!"

The Evocator in the west calls, "Abartala, we have prepared this Temple and have laid the foundation for your coming. Come now into this Triangle to speak with us and to grant us your power and knowledge. Abartala, come."

The Evocator in the north calls, "Abartala, we have prepared ourselves to see you, we have groomed ourselves to be in your presence. Grant us your presence now within this Triangle of Manifestation. Abartala, come."

The Evocator in the east calls, "Abartala, we have moved the heavens to call you here. The gods and the angels have made way for your coming. The devils and the demons have granted you passage into this world. Enter it now through this Triangle. Abartala, come."

The whole of the Temple will be in a state of rapture, as of Enoch quaking as it was lifted in the heavens. The conjuration as spoken above, backed by the power that fashioned existence, will call the spirit into being. Its presence will be felt, and often beheld by the inner eye, in the Triangle, forming a body that may be seen and heard, which may walk upon the earthen ground of the Temple.

A perfect calmness must be invoked and maintained through the ritual, the thoughts, and expectations of the participants tunneling towards the sole function of the inevitable materialization of the spirit. Even as the flood of omnipotence soars through the veins, the Operators' breathing should remain steady, their hearts beating without trepidation, their motions and their orations offered without quaver. The stillness, not only in one, two, or three Evocators, but in the whole group, will allow the powers of the rite to ride into this world unchained, opening through the Circle a nexion into the

Eternal. In the center of the Triangle, the first materializations of the spirit will usually be in the form of a white mist. This mist will initially be disregarded as the incense smoke, but as it continues to form it will be seen to be more solid, moving in and out of this plane, appearing as a type of steam which does not rise but remains perfectly centered in the Triangle and hovers two or three feet above the ground.

Recite in unison the basic calling that increases not only the materialization of the spirit, but also that rapture which threatens the conscious state of all present. "Abartala, come! Abartala, come! Abartala, come!" When working with a group, it is always interesting to note the various mechanisms by which each participant receives the vision of the spirit. Although Abartala is forming a body within the Triangle, he will connect with the minds of the Operators, filling their senses with specific and individual messages, personal statements or visions which few have every been known to recount after the ritual, and which is usually said to have entirely altered the individual's approach to his or her life. Also, just as the visions in the scrying device were obtained differently by each person, the spirit will be beheld differently in this evocation. However it manifests to those present, its manifestation should be verified by each person ceasing the repetitive incantation of, "Abartala, come."

The Evocator in the northern position is to greet the spirit in the usual manner, saying, "Abartala, we welcome you to this Temple, and we thank you eternally for answering our call and for your swift and full attendance."

Most entities, when evoked, will carry on two separate conversations. The first is the verbal conversation, which usually consists of the answering of questions and charges and general functional speech; the second conversation, however, goes largely unnoticed on a conscious level. The spirit will communicate silently with the Evocator, often without his awareness, either receiving thoughts and feelings from the Operator, or inserting foreign ideas that are usually dismissed as random and intrusive thoughts. Once the Magician is aware of such covert conversations, he may then learn to divide his attention likewise, both telling the spirit verbally that which he has put to memory for recital, and at the same time using the psychic link to enforce his desires and to commune with the evoked at a much deeper and lasting level. This mechanism of dual conversation is never noticed as clearly as when engaged in group evocation. It is also much more obvious when a spirit such as Abartala is evoked, whose entire function is to connect intellectually, psychically, and spiritually with the Operator.

It is easy to become lost in the internal conversations, allowing the spirit to guide and instruct without the restraint of words. Nevertheless, the ritual of evocation must meet its climax and must be completed in order to bring to full fruition the desires of the group. The southern Evocator is to give the command, "Abartala, we have summoned you here to start us on our path of Ascent together. We ask that you will guide us towards the first steps that we should take on this Path, that you will be a constant inspiration towards our mutual growth, and that your influence will move the four of us forwards and upwards at all times." After this formal request is made, any other participant may make individual requests, allowing the spirit time to respond to each if necessary.

After all conversation has concluded with Abartala, the northern Magician is to dismiss the spirit and end the ritual by stating, "Abartala, we thank you eternally for your attendance, and for the accomplishment of the tasks with which you have been charged. Go now into the world to bring to manifestation those things, armed with power and sealed with purpose. Abartala, you are dismissed."

Group Evocation 2

Activating an entire group of trained and developed Sorcerers for the evocation of an entity which could successfully be summoned by a single Evocator may seem superfluous, at best. The group evocation given above, while having merit that is evident in the solidity of the materialization of the spirit and the potency of the ritual altogether, serves its primary function of further uniting the members of the group spiritually and psychically. It allows a natural and spontaneous merger of minds and energies that will exponentially magnify all future workings. The meat of the matter, the forbidden art that is being revealed, the science which alchemists dare not name, is not only the rite of evocation utilizing multiple Summoners, but also utilizing multiple spirits to accomplish a single task. It is difficult for the average biped to even bring to imagination the experience of summoning to visible appearance a demon or angel, or to hear the reanimated voice of a long dead sage – to bring into this world in a concrete and verifiable manner that which is most surely not supposed to exist at all. Here, four Sorcerers face the same numbing awe in summoning to physical materialization two separate and distinct entities, with intellects, wills, emotions, powers, and abilities entirely their own, in the same moment, in the same Temple, for the same cause.

The Temple is arranged as before, with two exceptions: Two Triangles of Manifestation are inscribed on the ground, one in the north position and one in the south; and two altars are set in the Circle, one facing the north and the other facing the south. Each Triangle is to hold a brazier, the northern Triangle filled with frankincense incense and the other with pine incense. Each altar is to hold two black candles, a chalice filled with sweet wine, blood or saltwater, a ritual dagger, and any books or journals that may be necessary. The sigil of Tenebrion is placed in the center of the southern altar, and the sigil of Masphital in the center of the northern altar. These two entities, when summoned individually, permeate the air with a smothering darkness. When evoked together, it seems as if all of the hosts of hell wait, watching the summoning rite, ready to leap into battle at the hint of their Lords. Tenebrion and Mastiphal, not only being demonic entities, but carrying with them a darkness that is terrifying to presence, may not be suited to all Sorcerers. Some may be drawn towards the natural energies of the earth, and may choose to evoke Pirasca in the north, a spirit of water who appears riding a deep blue wave, surrounded by the sound of water, in collusion with Fuscar in the south, who is a fiery spirit who appears as a large spirit with a red tint to his skin and smoke rising from him. When Fuscar speaks, smoke issues from his lips as well, as if the inner parts of his being are constantly on fire.

Those Operators who are drawn more to the angels may evoke Andreafal from the north, who is a beautiful female angel carrying the essence of peace and well-being, and Exartal in the south who appears as an androgynous angel, said to be a lieutenant of the angelic armies under Michael, and is the exacter of the will of the Divine, voiced to him by Michael and carried out by Exartal's familiars in the physical plane. Finally, the Sorcerers who wish to work with planetary powers, the Jupiter Ian Prince Ablator may be summoned from the north, and Marisco, who is a female Mercurial spirit may be summoned from the south.

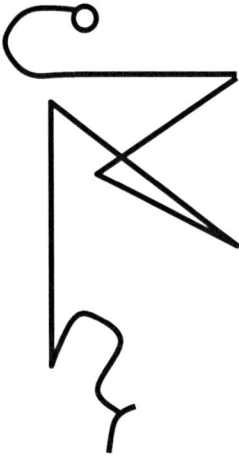

Tenebrion

Masphital

Pirasca

Fuscar

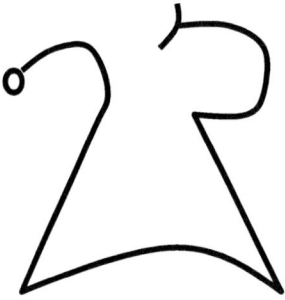

Andreafal

Exartal

Alator

Marisco

Any of these entities, when evoked simultaneously with their counterparts, will produce both an immediate and spontaneous effect on the Evocators' lives, as well as a combined potency in achieving the goals put to them. Their powers are not restricted to particular fields, but instead lie in their perfect command over their legions. The efficiency of their work on your behalf is made evident most when they are commanded to set into action armies of spirits, demons, angels, or familiars to achieve one goal.

Two Magicians stand at the northern altar to summon Masphital, the other two stand behind the southern altar to summon Tenebrion, or any of the other spirit combinations given above. Divinity and omnipotence is invoked by all participants in the same moment, and the altars and Triangles are consecrated by the Evocators governing that direction. The Circle is then consecrated by a single Sorcerer chosen beforehand.

Return to your places behind the altars once the initial consecrations have been completed. Turn the sigil of the spirit that you have come to summon upwards, and gaze into the sigil briefly until it begins to flash and your sight awakens into it, at which point you will quietly say, "In." When the same signal has been repeated by all, the Evocators in the south call out in unison: "Tenebrion, hear our voices, see our signs, and know that we command the universe to bring you before us, so that we may see you, so that we may hear you, and so that your power will be our power, your strength will be our strength, and your knowledge will be our knowledge."

Immediately after this oration is finished, the Evocators in the north answer it with, "Mastiphal, hear our voices, see our signs, and know that we command the universe to bring you before us, so that we may see you, so that we may hear you, and so that your power will be our power, your strength will be our strength, and your knowledge will be our knowledge."

The sigils are then touched by the Magicians evoking their chosen entity, and it is imbued with the power of the rite. As the energy and purpose fill the paper and transmute its fibers, the participants state in the direction of their sigil, "We seal this calling upon you, and we seal the power to perform this feat within this Temple in which you will manifest."

The ritual is to proceed as usual, with the two sets of Sorcerers scrying into and fully opening their separate sigils, and calling the entity through word and through will into the Temple. The spirit is guided as before towards the area of the Triangle in which it is to manifest. With the sets of spirits given above, the southern spirit is summoned forth through verbal conjuration, and once it begins to materialize within the Triangle, the northern spirit is called into materialization.

The spirits are then given the same command, which is to be recited in unison by the group, each to the spirit that he has summoned, yet the same words and the same task being given. The command given should be decided upon before the evocation is even planned, to ensure that it is one that will mutually benefit every member of the evocation group individually, as well as the party as a whole. The spirits are then likewise dismissed through verbal command given in unison.

The groups of spirits given above have been summoned in similar dual-evocation rituals thousands of times by thousands of Evocators. They have proven through centuries of trial to work most cooperatively, both with one another and also with the group of Magicians summoning them. It is ill-advised, at this early a juncture in multiple evocations, to begin throwing any two spirits together to evoke in the same ritual. Often, what will ensue will not be the anticipated powerful collaboration of entities and Sorcerers, but a spiritual and sometimes deadly battle for power. Just as no Magician who believes that he is at a greater or a lesser spiritual or moral standing than that of the entities with which he works can have complete success in evocation, the same counter-productivity is seen in an amplified form when two entities are summoned in the same Temple at the same time who feel that their strength must not be challenged, even if the challenge comes only from within. With experience, the names and the signs of spirits, which will work with one another to create exponential gain, will be given to the Evocator. Some of these are given in this chapter; more are given in those to come.

The basic formulae outlined in this chapter can be adapted for any number of Sorcerers and Sorceresses, as well as for up to four spirits. If the advise given above concerning the meshing of uncooperative spirits is not heeded, or often if more than four spirits are summoned together, and their spatial placing or other various factors are not made perfect, the participants will experience some of the most extreme spiritual and occult phenomenon of their lives, which will dazzle them and damage them for the remainder of their days. These works are forbidden with good cause. We are walking a line with these arts between annihilation and exaltation, and we must walk it with the greatest caution, yet also with the greatest passion to rise beyond limitation.

Chapter Eight
Multiple Evocations

After working with a group of Conjurers, the previously solitary Magician will find power and peace that had hitherto been undiscovered. It is always evidenced, however, that even though a group may work the miraculous together, and even though they may walk the earth as the unbreakable horsemen of the apocalypse, that this path is a personal one. It is an intimate union between the dying and the Eternal, between man and God. The experiences gained and the lessons learned in evoking and ritualizing as a group are integrated into the Operator's own personal path of Ascent, and with such a treasure, he or she continues down that path comfortably alone.

Having evoked with the formulas and the entities given in this book thus far, and having summoned multiple spirits in group ritual, the Evocator flexes new muscles with greater confidence, and takes that which has been gained into his Temple, again alone, into the shadows of creation, to be seated upon his unseen throne to rule his universe once more. A great understanding of the enlightened Masters is that Soul is the Absolute, experiencing itself finitely and subjectively; as such, the interactions that we have with one another are simply paths that we have created to experience ourselves in an objective manner. In the rituals of group evocation, we can see our partners as simply facets of ourselves that could not at that point be accessed through a single microcosm. Returning again to solitary practice, the Magician has Ascended above this need for externalization, and is therefore ready to invoke and to embody the collective energies that once required a group of four.

While group ritualization is beneficial and becomes extraordinarily comfortable, the Evocator begins to see it as a pretty thing, a novelty in which he will become immersed when his being seeks enjoyment. When it is power that he lusts, however, he will go alone into his Temple to draw the sword of the ages and to take dominion.

Consecutive Evocation

Evoking several entities in one ritual combines the powers, intelligence, and abilities of the entities summoned for one specific goal. When evoking a set of entities in a group ritual, although the power is exponentially multiplied, the phenomena of the Calling is enhanced, and the end results are achieved much more quickly and surely, the task and difficulty of the evocation is also shared with the other participants. Standing alone within the Circle, the solitary Evocator solely inherits the power and the results of the working, but he must further adapt his being to the spiritual pressurization of the Temple as the entities enter one by one, and to the enhanced rapture tending towards total fugue when he alone is the anchor which holds the heavens firmly to the earth. This spiritual and psychological adaptation is accomplished without losing the benefit of multiple evocation by evoking more than one entity, one at a time without breaks or pauses in between.

For any goal that you desire to achieve in your life and your growth, choose two entities to evoke. For these first experiments, it is best to summon entities whose nature is similar and whose powers are parallel. Analyzing the two entities, using the judgment developed through your own experience, discern which will be the easiest to summon to appearance, and summon that entity *after* the more challenging one. Two principles come into play when performing multiple evocations consecutively: The evocation of the first spirit creates a momentum that is carried into the evocation of the second spirit; and the physical and psychological states deteriorate steadily throughout the ritual, leaving the human being subjectively weakened the longer the ritual carries on. This is said to be the transfiguration of the dying man, his frail body giving way for the Godself to emerge. In rare cases, some of my associates and myself have found ourselves unconscious before the conclusion of a ritual, with all signs of the ritual having been completed, leaving us to wonder that if that fragile and dying being that we call "ourselves" is not present, who then is? Who finishes the ritual when we are dead, before we rise again in the flesh? While the Greater powers and intelligences that are possessed by the Godself or the Supersoul can act independent of our conscious mind for our own betterment, and often do with most situations in our lives (unknown to our oblivious and blinded minds), it is *conscious* contact with this undying power that is sought - thus we must struggle to remain conscious and alive throughout.

The actual ritual for such a consecutive evocation follows the exact pattern outlined in the fifth chapter of this text. When the first entity is commanded and dismissed, the evocation of the second entity begins without collection or hesitation, the likes of which will annihilate the momentum gained in the first evocation. The energy and omnipotent flow will be carried over from the first spirit to the second, and will bring the whole ritual to a fruitful conclusion.

The command given to both entities is to remain unchanged in letter and spirit, both entities working towards the same goals under the same exact direction.   However complex multiple evocations may become, the cardinal rule is to always evoke for a single cause.   Conflicting energies, whether they originate from entities who are summoned and who attempt to overthrow present reality with one energy current while another entity attempts to utilize the same Temple space and the same time, with the same ritual foundation as the other, or if the energy is generated by the Sorcerer himself, will often not only cancel each other out, but will do so in the spiritual equivalence of a reaction caused by atomic fusion.

One of my earliest and more ambitious students took to sigil Magick with great interest, and after handing him a certain potent and volatile grimoire, he began to consecrate sigil after sigil, opening pathways to spirits and energies for every problem and desire in his life. The next morning when I checked in on him, I found him sitting on his couch in his hooded robe, staring deep into absolutely nothing, unmovable from some induced trance. His roommate explained the previous night's rituals. After ridding the room of all of the energies that he had summoned, retiring the sigils in the prescribed manner, and giving him two days to sit and stare into his own stupidity, he returned to normal… and he never touched Magick again.

Rituals are given later in this chapter for the evocation of multiple entities whose nature seems rather contradictory, but whose *intent* is aligned. It is this power of intent that cannot be crossed. The Sorcerer must focus on one goal, and perform the rituals for that single goal, rather than attempting to accomplish all things at once.

The first solitary ritual of multiple evocation will seem surreal, the conscious mind not being ready to attempt the analysis of psychological impossibility. The experience will be assimilated, however, and the second or third such evocation will spring to life inside of the Evocator and will begin to change him and lift him above himself. His goals will be achieved with increased speed and efficiency, the space of time between his desire and the fulfillment of it closing. Soon, he will know that he is ready to move forward and upward, to grow even closer to his own Limitless nature.

Consecutive Evocations

The Operation of evoking two entities to stand around the Circle at once is no more complicated than the previous Working of evoking two entities consecutively, and may actually prove to be more natural and fluid, as none of the energy of the Operation is dispersed in sending one spirit away before calling the other. In actuality, the reverse is true: the greatest difficulty experienced with multiple evocation is the containment of the power summoned – the wherewithal to take the omnipotent forces flowing through you and channel them into the ritual, rather than allowing them to destroy you like any other weak and dying element.

The spirits Dumkaal and Fertaal are to be evoked in this manner before any other. They are called the Brothers of the Southern Winds, and they are quick to carry out any command from the Operator. They are especially adept in persuading people to conform to the will of the Magician. A single altar is placed within the Circle, facing south, holding the necessary tools. The two sigils of the entities evoked are placed face down in the center of the altar, the sigil to be used first being to the right and the second being placed to the left. One Triangle of Manifestation is placed in the southeast position, in which Dumkaal will manifest, and another is placed in the southwest position, in which Fertaal will manifest.

Braziers should burn in both Triangles, the incense of rose in the southeast Triangle and the scent of pine in the southwest.

All consecrations proceed as usual, and as Dumkaal will be the first spirit to be summoned, it is his Triangle that is consecrated first, and then Fertaal's. As multiple evocations become more complex, I will inscribe the name of the spirit in the Triangle in which he will materialize, to simply solidify in my mind that it is that place, and that place alone, in which the spirit will be able to arise.

Turn the sigil of Dumkaal face-up. Gaze into it for a moment and feel the initial connection between yourself and the spirit being established. Look up towards the southeast Triangle, in the empty space above it, and call, "Dumkaal, hear my voice, see my signs, and know that I command the universe to bring you before me, so that I may see you, so that I may hear you, and so that your power will be my power, your strength will be my strength, and your knowledge will be my knowledge." Take the ritual dagger in your right hand and with it touch the face of the spirit's sigil, allowing the omnipotent power to flow through the dagger into the parchment. State, "I seal this calling upon you, and I seal the power to perform this feat within this Temple in which you will manifest."

The same is done for the sigil and the initial calling of Fertaal. Both spirits will answer the call, and their presence will begin to seep into the Temple. In the same moment, the process of ascending rapture will initiate, a simple lightheadedness and shortness of breath heralding the first stages of the materialization of the spirits.

Looking towards the south, between both Triangles, take the chalice in your left hand and raise it above your head. Sense the power radiating from the fluid within, holding God tightly within the wine, ready to offer it only to the initiated. Call, "I drink the blood of God. I take within me all power." Bring the chalice to your lips and drink, feeling the elixir rush though your veins, conquering the exhaustion that has set in thus far, resurrecting the power and purpose of the ritual. Replace the chalice and begin to heap incense upon the braziers.

As the smoke fills the Temple, providing a thick air in which the spirits may materialize, place both hands upon the altar, palms down, on either side of the two sigils. Gaze at the sigil of Dumkaal and lock into your mind the still image of your desire. With your ritual dagger, trace the lines of the sigil on the paper and feel them springing to life. Transfer through your vision this desire into the paper. As the paper and the ink become transmuted into spirit, the entity that you are summoning will become irrefutably present. In the place of a mass of vaporous power, you will sense Dumkaal standing in the Temple, a spiritual giant waiting to be called into this plane. Once the sigil has been opened and Dumkaal is thus waiting, move your attention to the sigil of Fertaal, consecrating and opening it. Fertaal will likewise enter reality; the brothers of the southern winds waiting to be conjured.

The conjuration for this type of evocation is written and performed in a manner that will bring both entities into materialization simultaneously, rather than having Dumkaal materialize a body while Fertaal waits, and then have Dumkaal sit in the Triangle waiting for Fertaal to manifest. While it is easily assumed that bringing two entities into materialization at the same time is more difficult than doing so consecutively, the power generated by the ritual and the momentum created through the simultaneous evocation of the two spirits builds upon itself. It must be remembered that when the basic principles of evocation are adhered to, all of these things occur independent of the Magician. Magick is a chain reaction that begins at an unseen level and adjusts all things until the effect is achieved perfectly and solidly in the physical plane. Those who tamper with evocation without the pure purpose of will and without proper preparation to see and hear those things that they summon will indeed summon something that is beyond their comprehension, and the inevitable result is terrifying. Once the conjuration is spoken with will and with power, and the incense smoke thickens and the white mist begins to gather within the Triangles, there is no stopping the forces that have been set into motion. The single goal of the Evocator, at that point, is to hold fast to his consciousness and to his conviction to see the ritual through to the end.

Dumkaal   Fertaal

"Dumkaal, Fertaal, brothers of the southern winds, come forth into this world from the world beyond. I call you forth into these Triangles of Manifestation, into this Eternal Temple, into this plane of flesh and substance, to exercise power over this world and to exact dominion over its inhabitants, as you are instructed. Dumkaal, Fertaal, come now into the Temple and take your places within the Triangles. Dumkaal, Fertaal, come!"

As this conjuration is recited, the rapture of the Divine Power, which floods through you, will become unbearably intense. The dizziness brought by it will threaten your consciousness. Hold tight to the last vestiges of your mind as the spirits begin to take form in their Triangles. Breathe in slowly and feel both Triangles being inhabited by the spirits. Breathe out and sense their presence growing stronger and more solid. Continue your controlled breathing as they take their first materialized form in this world as mist, and begin coercing them through their names: "Dumkaal, Fertaal, come! Dumkaal, Fertaal, come!" Lift your ritual dagger into the air before you as you chant their names. Allow their names to possess you, to enrage you with the passion of their coming. Chant their names again and again until your mind is lost, until all that once was physical and dying is dead and you look out to the south and can see to either side the formation of the bodies of the brothers of the southern winds.

Guardians of the Watchtowers

The four cardinal points that we now have named north, east, south, and west have always been respected in religion and Magick. Every system of the occult and every church's dogma demonstrates the power of the physical world in spiritual matters. The great gates of Babylon were arranged according to these cardinal points. Christian prophecy is filled with reference to the directions, Christ coming from one cardinal point, Satan from another, the armies of the north invading the south, etc. Some anthropologists have offered amazing evidence of the arrangement of the Egyptian pyramids in a manner completely harmonious with each other in relation to the cardinal directions. And in each of the world's systems through time, these directions that seemed so solid and objective did not stand alone but were ruled over by the Guardians of the Watchtowers. Modern, New Age Magick teaches the importance of these Watchtowers and their Guardians, but fails to fully recognize their nature as solid, immovable entities who can be called forth into physical materialization just as surely, if not more so due to their inherent connection with the earth plane, than any other spirit.

The names and faces of the Guardians of the Watchtowers change from one Aeon to another and from one system to another, but their powers remain the same – although some have been diminished while others have been exalted through time. Even though it is difficult to dispute the potency of the coming of the four Archangels of the Directions, their raw force seems to pale once the Sorcerer has summoned cardinal guardians whose names have been called since man could first speak. Beings such as the Mayan guardians Ix, Cauac, Kan, and Mulac, who have been called through the most ancient and often the bloodiest rites, shake the foundations of reality as they enter it.

For the purpose and function of learning to summon the guardians of the watchtowers, the aforementioned Archangels will be evoked as the first exercise: Raphael to the east, Michael to the south, Gabriel to the west, and Uriel to the north. If demonic energies and entities are more comfortable, the four Demonic Kings of the cardinal points: Satan, Beelzebub, Azazel, and Astaroth can be evoked instead of the archangels, Beelzebub to the east, Satan to the south, Azazel to the west, and Astaroth to the north.

Arrange the Temple with a Triangle in each of the cardinal points and a single altar in the exact center of the Circle. The altar should face south for the demonic kings and north for the archangels, and is to hold the sigils of the four entities, face down, arranged on the altar in the same position they will hold in the Temple. Different incenses may be used in each of the censors, although a single scent will work for the materialization just as well.

Begin the ritual, and as before, include the names of each of the Guardians in the orations. When the time has come to consecrate and open the sigils, do so from east and clockwise for the angels or south and counterclockwise for the demons, opening each sigil until the entity is within the Temple waiting to come into manifestation, turn to face the next Triangle and consecrate that sigil, until all are flashing with power and the spirits await. Collect yourself for a moment before continuing, sensing the collective presence of the Guardians of the Watchtowers, feeling their diverse powers and intelligences filling the air. Often, with an evocation as intense as this, their voices may be heard as if in the wind, or the room might begin to flash with nearly imperceptible lights as the balancing energies of the cardinal points come into full manifestation.

Two sets of conjurations are given for the summoning of the Guardians of the Watchtowers into physical materialization, a Grand Conjuration that calls the collective entities into this world, and specific conjurations that focus on the materialization of each entity separately. As the Grand Conjuration is spoken, turn either clockwise or counter-clockwise, depending on the entities that you summon, and give the call to each direction equally.

"Guardians of the Watchtowers, I call you forth into this Temple in beholdable form and in perfect visage. I call you into this world to speak to me and to ravage the earth with your power. Guardians of the Watchtowers, you are conjured into physical form and comprehensible likeness. Guardians of the Watchtowers, I call you forth. Guardians of the Watchtowers, rise!"

During the speaking of the conjuration, and after it is spoken in the silent moment, release your own imperfect will the to the Will of the ritual itself, to that power which lingers just beyond the ego's grasp, and with that omnipotent union between the human will and the Divine Will, direct the Guardians to rise up from the dust and the smoke and to enter this world. The Guardians will begin to take form around the Circle within their Triangles, the incense smoke thickening as a brilliant white mist and their features flashing in the air as they solidify on this plane. While they are in the process of materialization, turn to the east or the south, respectively, and give the conjuration of that spirit.

"(Spirit's name), I call you and conjure you forth to stand in this Temple and to take your place within the Triangle. I summon you to manifest before me in beholdable form and to speak with me in a discernable voice. (Spirit's name), I give you license to appear, I give you power to manifest, I give you this call to come. (Spirit's name), come!"

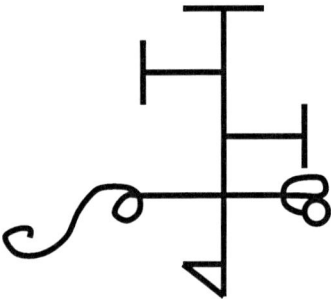 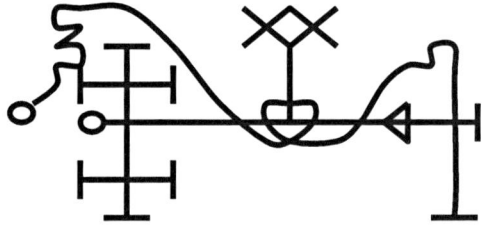

Raphael   Michael

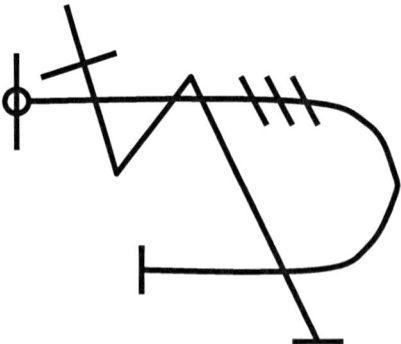 

Gabriel   Auriel

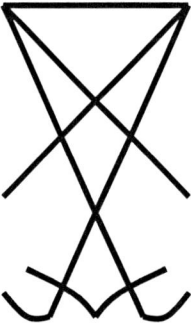

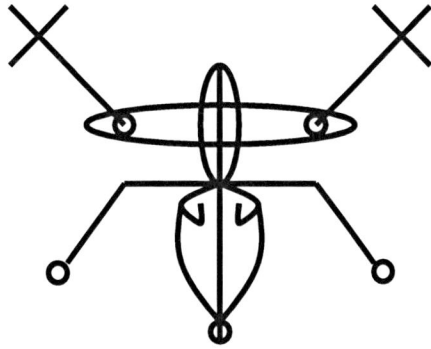

Satan   Beelezbub

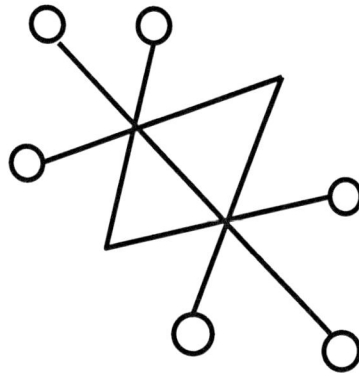

Astaroth   Azazel

    The first spirit will begin to construct a body from the fine particles of the ether, and as the white mist in the Triangle solidifies, you are to turn to the next Triangle and give the same conjuration to that spirit. Rotate in a complete circle either clockwise or counterclockwise, returning to the first spirit conjured. Repeat the phrase, "Guardians of the Watchtowers come!" Their manifestations will become more concrete, and the whole of the Operation will seem to take a more chaotic tone than any before. Their bodies will flicker violently in and out of view, their voices will rumble and clamor as the come into the world, and their powers will soar through the Temple and mingle directly above the altar.

When all four Guardians stand within their Triangles, slowly spin in your place to address them all, giving your command to them equally. Through this process you will sense a definite and undeniable battle of will, the conflicting energies struggling to remain balanced, and in that struggle trapping you, the Operator, in the apex of power. You must be the centrifuge of the forces which fly, pulling them together and at the same time asserting your absolute will into the ritual and into the intent of the Guardians. They will crumble universes if such is the true will of the omnipotent Sorcerer, once the clamor of conflict is stifled and the Temple is balanced by the Magician's will.

Conflicting Nature/Aligned Intent

The final Operation of multiple evocation is the summoning forth of entities whose intrinsic natures are in complete conflict, yet their natural intent or the Divine Providence of their creation is in complete alignment. A great example of this is the archangel Raphael, the Divine Physician, and the Goetic President Marbas. One is a Sephirotic and godly archangel, sworn by his very existence to do only that which will lift man into the eternal love of God, and the other is a demon who is said to work for the sole purpose of the destruction of men's souls. Both, however, have also been created by the Eternal Source of All Things to heal the body, mind, and heart of man. The angel and the demon do not cooperate with one another begrudgingly, but instead both go to work on the goal that has been presented to them as if the other entity is not involved in the Operation in the least. The benefit of this type of evocation is that each type of entity will work towards the goal in a different way. Raphael will cultivate the energy of his Sephiroth, as well as pure Divine energy, in the patient, thus healing the malady. Marbas will bring the base energies, often from the earth itself and from the patient's Root Chakra, into full activity in the healing process. This combination produces the miraculous.

Using the methods given in this chapter for the evocation of multiple entities by one Operator, any number of entities of diverse alignment and natures can be summoned for one goal, so long as their inherent intent is aligned with the others.

Chapter Nine
Evoking Legions

I saw a painting when I was about sixteen years old of a young Sorcerer crouched in a shadowed cavern. He held in his right hand a sword that radiated power, and in his left hand he held a leather-bound grimoire. Legions of demons stood around him, shrieking in the darkness from the power of the Sorcerer's Magick, yet eyes unable to waiver from his sight. I cannot recall the artist or the title of the piece, but the image will never leave my mind. It impressed upon me the power that one might have, if only they dare uncover the secret teachings of Magick, and dare even more to uncover the hideous and glorious beings that hide behind the veils of the senses.

For a very long time I thought back on that painting as a symbolic thing, as a metaphor of the power of man. Even while gaining mastery over evocation, I could not see the literal essence of it. Ironically, the first two times that I had performed an evocation which spontaneously brought about the materialization of seemingly countless entities at once, I still did not think that a person – specifically myself – could summon to physical manifestation, constrain, and command legions of spirits at once. The Operation must have gone wrong somewhere, I thought. Perhaps the admonitions of the authors of the ancient grimoires were correct, and I had somehow unwittingly opened a forbidden gateway into some

155

unknown realm and had let the hordes flood into this world. At the close of the ritual, however, with the execution of a dispelling oration, every last spirit fled back through the gateway into their original world, and the goal of the evocation was achieved exactly as instructed and in unbelievable time. In analyzing these occurrences, however, I began to see an obvious system by which legions may be summoned.

Thus far, sigils have been used to link the mind of the Operator to the essence of the subject. Even when evoking multiple entities, each one must be called using its sigil and name as a definite connection to that one spirit. The elementary principle of creating and sustaining substantial contact with the spirit in the evocation ritual must be always be satisfied in order to bring into full manifestation the entity or entities that you have chosen. This principle is in no way invalidated by the fact that several, if not countless entities are being summoned in one Magickal gust. The ritual, therefore, simply needs to be modified to fulfill this principle of evocation and facilitate the mass manifestation, by establishing substantial contact with the group of entities rather than with each individual spirit, connecting to the collective rather than the independent spirit.

Magick Squares

One of the most basic rituals that I've discovered for summoning forth legions of spirits is the opening of certain Magick squares.

Magick squares are squares containing either numbers or letters that have perfect numerological significance. They have been known for certain to exist for at least 4,000 years in various cultures and religions, always being used as forms of talisman or amulet Magick. Although mathematicians have studied the mathematical significance of those squares which have appeared in ancient grimoires, and art connoisseurs have attempted to dissect the beauty of the things, it is only the Adept who has opened the squares and experienced them as living things who have uncovered the hidden geometry of the squares, the numbers, the angles, and the words.

Magick squares act much like sigils, with the exception that they naturally produce a much more broad and sweeping effect in the immediate environment, in the psychic realms of communication and connection, and in the end results. The square serves as a nexion into a very specific region and function of the spiritual universe, linking the Temple with that region, uniting the Temple and it totally and calling into full activity its powers and influence. In the majority, Magick squares have been used as a sort of folk Magick, in which the square is drawn on paper, wax, wood, or some other surface, and is considered to affect its Magick by the very drawing of it. While the symbol may have a good deal of power in itself, when the Magician learns to fully open the square as a gateway into the beyond, and learns to either travel through it into another plane, or to call other entities to travel through it into this plane, the square is known to be a multi-dimensional portal whose applications are seemingly endless.

Some Magick squares will summon into the Temple a massive influx of power directed at one specific final result, while others will indeed call into physical materialization hordes of spirits to answer the call and to hear the Sorcerer's command. In all actuality, I have yet to find any distinguishing marks between the two by any method or science outside of putting into practice the ritual of opening the squares. In that ritual, which is given below, I have included two squares that have produced the latter effect and will provide you with the tools necessary to summon forth legions by this method.

The Temple is prepared in the uniform manner for evocation, save for the placement of any Triangle. The outside of the Circle is left free for the spirits to inhabit as they will, and eight censors surround the Circle to provide enough manifestation base for the spirits to materialize. The incense should be pine, cedar, or another coniferous resin, producing a forest-like scent in the Temple. The altar should face north and a chair should be set behind it, as the Operator here will be seated throughout the Operation, rather than standing as in traditional evocation. The arrangement of the altar does not vary from that used in the ritual of evocation, the dagger and chalice in their places, as well as two white candles on the edge of the altar and the square in the center, drawn on a piece of five inch by five inch parchment. As in every ritual Operation, any written materials which aide in the evocation may be placed on or around the altar, as well as a notebook or journal in which the events may be recorded.

The first square, which will be ritually opened, is given in The Book of the Sacred Magic of Abramelin the Mage, third book, fifth chapter, and first square, named Anakim, or Giants.

A	N	A	K	I	M
N					
A					
K					
I					
M					

The initial invocations and consecrations proceed as usual. Take your seat behind the altar, facing north, and turn the square face up. Gaze into it for a moment and feel the initial connection between yourself and the spirit being established. Sense a thousand eyes looking at you through the square, a thousand voices calling back through it, a thousand bodies waiting to take form in the Temple at your command. Look around the Temple at the empty spaces and call, "Anakim, giant spirits, hear my voice, see my signs, and know that I command the universe to bring you before me, so that I may see you, so that I may hear you, and so that your power will be my power, your strength will be my strength, and your knowledge will be my knowledge." Take the ritual dagger in your right hand and with it touch the face of the square, allowing the omnipotent power to flow through the dagger into the parchment. State, "I seal this calling upon you, and I seal the power to perform this feat within this Temple in which you will manifest."

Sense the number of entities beginning to fill the Temple. The sense of suffocation that is felt in evocation will here become more pronounced. You will feel much like you are in a small elevator with a lot of noisy people. The rapture will also come more quickly. It is not rare for the Sorcerer to begin to doubt himself in this Operation, not only the first time he performs it, but nearly every time that he sits in ritual to summon legions of spirits. Quell this feeling, refocus your intentions, and proceed.

Take the chalice in your left hand and raise it above your head. Call, "I drink the blood of God. I take within me all power." Bring the chalice to your lips and drink, feeling the elixir rush though your veins, conquering the exhaustion that has set in thus far, resurrecting the power and purpose of the ritual. Replace the chalice and begin to heap incense upon the braziers, moving in a clockwise manner.

As the smoke fills the Temple, providing a thick air in which the spirits may materialize around you, place both hands upon the altar, palms down, on either side of square. This simple physical uniting of your body with the altar, which is the base of the ritual, the Divine Rapture will increase, and the spirits will be senses even nearer. Gaze at the square deeply and lock into your mind the still image of your desire – not the appearance of the spirits, but the end result of the Working. With your ritual dagger, trace the lines of the square on the paper and feel them springing to life. Transfer through your vision this desire into the paper. As the paper and the ink become transmuted, the entities, which you are summoning, will become irrefutably present. The square will also be perceived to literally "open" as a gateway into the resident world of the spirits that you are calling. Where this simple square is composed of the same name, "Anakim," written twice, once vertically and once horizontally, your vision will bring one of these lines into sparkling reality while the other fades, and returns likewise. With more complex squares, they will disappear one at a time and reappear accordingly. It is important to write down the words in the order in which they reappear, unless you are able to remember them exactly. Often, the disappearance and reappearance of letters will seem to take no semblance of organization at all, once they are written down and repeated in the ritual, they will provide an added power that cannot be replaced or replicated by any other means. It is said that this is the manner in which the square speaks to you, guiding you and giving you the tools that you need to perform the evocation. I have had entire sentences, often given in the Enochian language, that once I had translated provided me exact guidance in my own path of Ascent for the following months, as well as prophesying that which would occur in that time. In the actual materialization, you will repeat these verbally as they manifested on the paper, and those will be the words and names that will cause the whole of the ritual to reach its summit.

The conjuration for this type of evocation needs to be adapted to the specific entities that you are calling. For this particular evocation, eyes still gazing into the square, you will recite: "Anakim, Giant Spirits, I summon you forth from the abyss into this Temple. I call you into this world to take form before me, to appear in bodies that I may see, to speak in voices that I may hear, and to assist me in (*state your goal in general terms*). Spirits, come!"

Gaze still locked into the open square, repeat, "Anakim, Anakim, come!" When you are using other squares, you will repeat the names and words as you had written them down when charging and opening the square, followed by the command, "come!" after the whole list has been named. This will be illustrated in the next exercise of evoking legions through squares.

As you call with repetition for the spirits to manifest, allow your senses to attune to them, seeing their massive forms taking shape around you. Look at the incense and see it turning a bright white, becoming the white mist rather than the gray smoke, going through the first stage of materialization. Here, the rapture will become unbearable. Your senses will seem to depart from this world and you will feel as if you are somewhere else entirely. Metaphysically, it becomes impossible to distinguish between your physical Temple and the spiritual home of the spirits that you are evoking. It is at this departure from known reality and consciousness that the spirits will take frightening form around you. I use the word "frightening" because I have yet to evoke legions of spirits and experience any emotion other than terror at this juncture of the evocation. As the entities begin to materialize, the speed at which they appear will grow more and more chaotic. The room will bustle with sound and will become crowded with the images of faces looking on, arms reaching out, the smells will fill the air and often make you gasp. You will feel as if the entire Operation has been taken out of your hands and now belongs to the spirits. Allow the materialization to finish, despite the giants that might be pounding the floor to get inside of the Circle, despite the demons that shriek your nightmares into your ears, despite the archangels who blow their trumps and threaten the wrath of god. Sit in your state of rapture and allow the process of materialization to run its course.

You will notice a definite slowing or sudden cease of the manifestations. It is as this point that you will stand and filled with omnipotence, give your command for all entities to stop and to hear your voice, and to obey.

These spirits, being some of the mightiest familiars a Sorcerer can ever summon, are capable of carrying out any minor task the Evocator may desire. Because of the number of spirits working on your behalf, you will see your results not only coming about more quickly, but also more closely to your exact specifications than before. With this method of evoking legions, I was able at one point to name an exact amount of money that I needed, and not only did I receive the whole amount (which was in the thousands) in less than forty-eight hours, but the amount I received nearly three hundred dollars more than I had requested!

Give your command in specific terms and dismiss the entities as usual. This last step is one of the most difficult to perform. Bringing legions of spirits into this world in physical bodies and willful intelligences is difficult enough, but then asking them to kindly depart is nearly impossible, and usually requires an unusual amount of raw will and spiritual authority. Take a moment, after having dismissed them, to collect yourself, to regain your focus, and to stand and to command them, with the omnipotent force that is within you, to return to whence they came and to do that which they have been commanded or requested to do. You may also recite the following incantation or banishing which will further rid the Temple of all entities and energies:

Ashtu malku ta dat arkata
Sastus seckz altamu partu
Iretempal krez ta felta
Vaskalla regent met senturus
Ta sastrus estos melta
Kelta, kelta, ketla hine.

The second square, which you will open and use for the evocation of multiple spirits, is an entirely forbidden usage of the Enochian Tablets, merging aspects of the element of fire with that of air, creating an unstoppable rain of flames from heaven to achieve a single magnificent goal. Elemental seniors and angels will spill into the Temple, merging these two polar elements in one space and time, creating an explosion by spiritual fusion, which will destroy all things with brimstone, and fire, after which all things may be created anew. This Operation is dangerous to employ, and it is said that the square itself is dangerous to even look upon unless the Operator has been prepared for immediate Ascent.

The Operation is conducted by the exact same parameters as the previous one, substituting only the square, the conjuration, and the names and words repeated during the materialization of the entities.

The conjuration is as follows:

Oh mighty Spirits of the Great Art of Union, oh Grand Angels of the Divine Law, enter now into this Temple as witnesses of the Universal Decree. Fill this Temple wall to wall and hear the voice that commands all things. Come now into this Temple. Come now into this world. Come now from your palaces of wind and flame and answer the call of the Eternal.

Heaping incense upon the braziers and thus filling the Temple with enough smoke to give base for the materialization of the spirits, begin to chant the words and names that appeared while opening the square. This very recital will bring to life that which once was null and will cause the spirits to rise from the dust in beholdable image before you.

A roaring may be heard as the spirits enter the Temple, as of a furnace churning with heat and flame in the moments before it bursts. As they materialize fully before you, you will sense – if not be completely overwhelmed by – the struggle to balance the opposing forces that are summoned. The battle will not be one between the spirits themselves, but between their inherent powers and energies. As before, wait, filled with omnipotence and swooning in rapture, and the universe will balance itself.

This specific ritual of evoking legions through this square is to be used for only the most pure goals, and only those that such a mega-powerful source such as this will do. Those acolytes who have previously put the Enochian system to use in their lives and in their

Ascent will likely stray from this square altogether, and will rightfully warn others to do the same. The greatest tool and weapon sits in your hands, on the altar, within the Circle and just outside of its boundaries. We can either use our arsenal to destroy ourselves to the point of eternal winter, we can pull the sun just close enough to boil the oceans, or we blossom Eden in our own lives.

This same ritual may be used for the opening of any square, although not every one will bring forth legions. Most will, in fact, bring into this world an intangible, invisible force that can shake the earth and bring the skies to flames. It is necessary to research each square thoroughly, to discover through numerology and etymology what exactly you are calling through that portal into this world. Using known numerological/phonetic systems such as Hebrew, numbered squares can be converted into letters, and can then be translated and deciphered. Knowing your enemies is important, but knowing your friends is vital. You must act as a wise and tempered Lord and all creation will bow before you.

House of Spirits

Another method that I've discovered for summoning legions in one ritual with one conjuration is the use of what I have termed a "house sigil," which calls upon a group of similar entities to appear together. A house sigil can be seen in much the same way as a coat of arms. It identifies a specific "bloodline" of entities that work and act together in one goal, whose existent natures are aligned, composing a "house of spirits." Often, when the Sorcerer summons an entity to do some difficult task, that entity will work with those in its "house" to accomplish the goal. What this creates is cooperation not only between a large number of spiritual dignitaries, but also between all of the familiar and subordinate spirits of each. This type of collusion is noticed the strongest with the demonic.

A house sigil is usually a derivation of or similar to the individual sigil of the entity who presides over the house, who will usually manifest with the group, taking the most solid form, and usually speaking for the group. If this does not happen, the presiding entity will often send a speaker or representative, sometimes disguised as the head of the house of spirits, only recognized to be any other by intuitive discernment or by intimate knowledge of the mannerisms of the particular spirit. House sigils which do not resemble the sigil of any one particular spirit are usually rather ornate and sometimes pictorial. It is posited that the seals given in the grimoire <u>The Black Pullet</u> and other such pseudo-sigils given in various Magickal texts throughout time, which do not seem to fit the classical design of entity sigils but rather have been classed as amulets or talismans are such house sigils.

The ritual of evocation using house sigils only slightly differs from the previous evocation ritual

The ritual exercise for this sort of evocation is that of the Mercurial spirits of the House of Kel. Medicine and intricate mechanics are expertly known by these spirits, but their greatest power is in their ability to influence automatic and instantaneous healing in any aspect of existence. At first sight, this may appear extremely useful only if you are ill or depressed, but if you objectively consider your whole existence, you may find that many things are in need of healing. You may have a sick financial situation, a splintered relationship, an infected and terminal career, or dying connection with your highest spirituality. Rather than acting like most entities do and influencing that which is not there to manifest in your life, the spirits of the House of Kel bring into full health that which is there. Nothing in life is truly broken, but simply may be presently manifesting in a weaker or immaturely developed form, and needs to be nurtured until your life flows with abundance.

The Temple is without a Triangle of Manifestation. Nine blue candles surround the Circle to provide enough manifestation base for the spirits to materialize, and three censers form a perfect Triangle in the Temple, one in the north, one in the southwest and the last in the southeast. Frankincense is the scent that should be burned for the evocation of the spirits of the House of Kel. The altar should face north and a chair should be set behind it. The arrangement of the altar remains the same, the dagger and chalice in their places, as well as two white candles on the edge of the altar and the sigil of the House is drawn on a piece of five inch by five inch parchment.

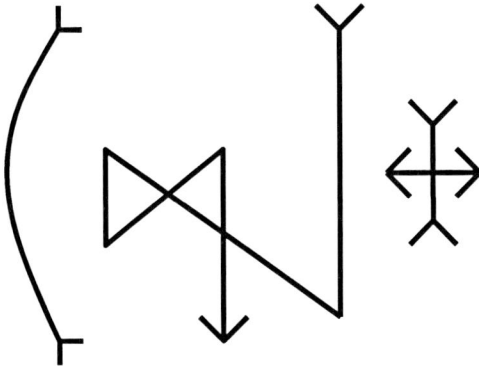

The normal invocations and consecrations open the ritual, after which you are to take your seat behind the altar, facing north, and turn the sigil face up. Gaze into it for a moment and feel the initial connection between yourself and the spirits of Kel being established. Sense them becoming aware of you, knowing your purpose and beginning to answer your unspoken call. Look around the empty Temple and call, "Spirits of the House of Kel, under the sign of Hod, come now and hear my voice, see my signs, and know that I command the universe to bring you before me, so that I may see you, so that I may hear you, and so that your power will be my power, your strength will be my strength, and your knowledge will be my knowledge." Take the ritual dagger in your right hand and with it touch the face of the sigil, forcing the omnipotence that has been invoked in you to rise into the blade and pass into the paper. State, "I seal this calling upon you, and I seal the power to perform this feat within this Temple in which you will manifest."

Sense the entities filling the Temple. Whereas previously the associated feeling was of suffocation, these spirits will usually bring light and lightness to the Temple, seeming to expand the space and to brighten the air, healing all things as they enter this world. In fact, it is the sanctity that they carry with them that will cause the needed rapture to reach its peak in you.

Meditate upon the spirits, seeing them in your mind and hearing their mental voices in the air, and when the psychological fugue begins to cause you to swoon, take the chalice in your left hand and raise it above your head. Call, "I drink the blood of God. I take within me all power." Bring the chalice to your lips and drink, feeling the fluid replenish you. Replace the chalice and begin to place incense upon the braziers, moving in a clockwise manner until the Temple is filled with smoke.

Return to your seat behind the altar and place both hands upon the altar, palms down, on either side of the sigil. Gaze at the sigil and bring to mind image of that which needs healing. With your ritual dagger, trace the lines of the sigil and transfer through the dagger your power and through your vision your desire into the lines on the paper. Begin to scry into the sigil in the normal manner, and as you do so you may notice that some of the entities will take quasi-solid manifestations around you, coming into this plane and then fading again, trying to break the veil between the worlds without your full assistance. More spirits will enter the Temple as you open the sigil as well, being called by the consecration of it.

When the sigil has been opened and all of the spirits wait, recite the conjuration that will bring them forth. "Spirits of the House of Kel, under the sign of Hod, guided by the great Archangel Michael, I summon you forth from the your swift sphere. I call you into this world to take form before me, to appear in bodies that I may see, to speak in voices that I may hear, and to assist me in (*state your goal in general terms*). Spirits of the House of Kel, come!"

Lock your gaze into their sigil, transfixed by it as if it will not allow your eyes to part, pulled into the lines and circles and empty white spaces, and repeat, "Spirits of the House of Kel, come!" Allow the rapture to build, and allow the spirits to take form as they will, and they will. The spirits of Mercury are quick to enter this world, and often will attempt to do so by various means outside of evocation. You will sense a great number of entities around you, all wanting badly to help you, all clamoring on top of one another to give you aide.

Look up from the sigil and continue to repeat the call for them to manifest. See with your eyes their bodies taking form, their shining faces joyous to see you, the incense smoke rising and turning to white light as it creates a body of flesh out of spirit. Here again, the rapture will become unbearable. Your senses will seem to depart from this world and you will feel as if you have stepped onto the glorious surface of Hod itself, rather than safe and sane at home on earth. The emotional and psychological state caused by the evocation along with the sight of the countless spirits filling the Temple forces your mind into collapse, and it is here that your mind will remove itself and that you must rely on your greater understanding and your higher senses to continue. It is also at this point that the spirits will take on a form more concretely physical and more astoundingly real than ever before.

If a particular entity shows itself to be the head of the House of Kel, which in this case is usually going to be an angelic minister, it will present itself or will instantly be known by the Operator.

Address the host of spirits with your desires for healing in your life, keeping with one specific goal rather than asking that they heal every aspect of your existence at once. It is also important to remember that they cannot heal that which is not ill, and if you attempt to deceive them in greed or lust for that which you already possess enough of, that very thing will grow weak and will wither by the force of a medicine that becomes a poison when it is not needed.

Dismiss the spirits and allow them to leave as they will without any banishing. Often, they will begin their work immediately, and may remain in the Temple for a few minutes after they are dismissed to do so.

Summoning as the Servant

Struggling for some semblance of balance on my path of Ascent, and attempting to deliver myself from the depths of the Dark Night of the Soul which had held me in absolute spiritual blackness for nearly seven years, around March of 2001 I burned all of the bridges that I had built with the sinister groups and subcultures over the years, resigned my position as Reverend High Priest of a notorious Demonic Church, and gained membership in the Sacred Order of the Son of God, a quasi-Christian Order whose works are derived directly from the Masonic Temple rites with strong occultic ties and Promethean doctrines of self-godhood through struggle. Being a religious order rather than strictly an occult order, ritual was replaced by prayer and invocation, and carrying over that which I had learned through evocation, spiritual travel, and the many other esoteric arts that I had studied over the years, I learned to use the tool of prayer and blessing in a substantial way. I would spend hours kneeling on my tile floor reading and re-reading and putting to memory the Book of John, catching myself up into the heavenly rapture that would lift me from this body and this earth into the realm of prophetic vision and angelic communion. I became a fanatic and at times a hermit, preferring the company of the brilliant white light that filled my room and the choirs of angels to any human sociality. In actuality, it was this maddening state of isolation and religious commitment to Ascent which brought my own faculties of Seership into full bloom, and which annihilated my fear of confronting supposed impossibilities.

Having retired for this period of spiritual reawakening to a simple life of virtually no overage in wealth or monetary gain, working only to pay for humble room and board and nothing more, I would put my free time towards deep meditation and prayer, often seeking out remote places where I could supplicate God, his Son, the Holy Spirit, and all of the angels for a closer union with that Divinity, and a closer connection with the aspects of the Spirit, Christ, and the Grand Architect within myself. A shallow river ran through a particular desert ravine in the rural outskirts of my hometown, and in walking along it I discovered a sandy island big enough to seat a single person. That island became one of my favorite meditation spots, away from society and the busy world with nothing but the sound of water running over sandstone rocks and the feel of the rising vapors as the summer sun melted away at the flowing river.

In the few years preceding this religious conversion that I had spent in deep Satanic and demonic studies, I had learned to summon, to view, and to effectively communicate with diverse entities, focusing my attention mainly on demons and pre-Judaic archetypes. Crossing over, I merged this ability with my newfound "faith" and, ridding myself of disbelief in the face of my fanaticism, had called upon the angels and had had them manifest to me, usually either through internal vision or, if they manifested physically, a single angel would descend to minister as it would. I had done away with incense smoke and candle flame, and so the solidity of the materializes that I was able to produce was diminished, not to mention the ability to materialize legions as I had before.

I knelt on my tiny island retreat with my back straight and my airways open, and began my meditation with simple controlled breathing and positive contemplation. I held in my mind an image of the desire for which I was beseeching the Divine and then called out the name, "El Shaddai," as I would often address the incomprehensible Source, and I began to pray. The oration flowed from me as if the words existed deep within or high above myself, and only in that moment was I ready to be the mouthpiece of the Divine. I remember feeling myself tremble and my eyelids flutter as the power and intelligence that is, by its own nature, everything rushed into the nothingness of the mortal shell that I assumed to be me. I cannot, however, remember the exact words that came from my mouth, aside from the development of humility through the salutary part of the prayer, the establishing of my authority to call upon the name of God and to command the hosts of heaven on His behalf through the Sacred Priesthood which was conferred upon me by the Order, and the calling upon ministering angels.

I had become entirely lost in my prayer, not concerned about the river or the island or the world at all, but drifting in an ocean of love and power wherein all that existed was myself, God, and the words of the prayer… and then the angels. The wind started blowing lightly, brushing the hot air across me as it would do during my meditations, and died completely in seconds. Still praying, I opened my eyes to find my vision not at all how it was previously. All around me the air was steaming with the white mist that is usually only seen in grey incense smoke at the moment that the spirits begin to materialize, rising up from the river around me and lingering at my eyelevel. Rather than simply coagulating into dense shapes that then form visible bodies, a unique white light shined into the mist and filled each particle of it with its brightness. Seemingly from the centers of each particle of mist, the bodies of the angels which I petitioned. Seeing this before me, my prayer of faith for a future occurrence took on the form of an acknowledgement of a present happening. I called, "El Shaddai, grant me the ministering of angels. Grant me the ministering of angels. Grant me the ministering of angels!" In the heat of the pounding sun and the automatic evocation that was taking place, I could feel my body swaying and my mind begging to not bear witness, to retreat into blackness and forget. I held the rapture tight, yet held closer to me the will to complete the materialization.

Two or three feet off of the surface of the water, the angels materialized, appearing to be kept in the air by a steady up-sweeping wind, although the air around me was completely still. When the entirety of them had manifested, floating above me in the middle of the day, seen by my eyes as clearly as any person, numerous voices emanated from the angel nearest me, who was also the first to materialize. The voices sounded like singing, although the words were unmistakably clear, asking how they could serve.

Others have had similar experiences, although few are ever able to duplicate it or even view it under the microscope of the metaphysical sciences to allow it to assume a reproducible form. Most who have been visited by angelic or some other benevolent, deific entities either experience the whole thing as an hallucination that can be easily rejected or they simply accept it as a once-in-a-lifetime visitation marking a turning point in their spiritual paths. I rather chose to view it as a turning point in all of existence, in the Supreme Conscious, and my ability to access that intelligence and omnipotence to produce real effect in the world. Rather than leading me deeper into the religion which sparked the fanaticism that had made the spontaneous evocation possible, this was in actuality one of the three steps which led me out of religion entirely and into unique and personal spiritual experiences that eventually showed me with my own eyes all that I once relegated to blind faith and dead hope.

Very few who have experienced the above type of manifestation have also taken the unwritten formulae and applied it to entities and deities as they will, with the same remarkable results.

The path of Ascent is your path and no one else's. It does not belong to any religion or any Savior. It does not belong to any archetype, or even to the Eternal Source. It is the way and the road that *you* consciously decide to travel, step-by-step, into your own limitlessness. Whether the road itself is paved with ivory or paved with brimstone is merely reflective of the needs of the individual who is experiencing Eternity for himself, by whatever means and methods he or she sees fit. The formula for evoking legions through prayer is simple, if there are no blockages to the will of the Evocator in doing so. The two great twin blockages are named Doubt and Fear; without them, limitations fade in the presence of the Adept. A potent tool for the elimination of doubt and fear from the sanctity of the Temple is absolute knowledge of the only possible result achievable by the process and formula that you apply. By this time, you should have already proven to yourself through your Workings that all that was once beyond possibility now is only a ritual away from attainment. Where spirits once were silent, now they roar. Where once they were unseen, they now rise up embodied before you. All that has changed in this process is the elimination of fear and doubt through experiences and results that you can hold in your hands and put in your pocket. This absolute knowledge, which when observed by the neophyte is called faith, must arise on its own, seeded by the Godlike nature of man and nurtured by his experience in acting as God... and having existence react in turn.

The tool for this type of evocation is often called prayer by the pious, but is often referred to by occultists as invocation, oration, or orison. The oration does not need to be directed towards any deity or archetype whose nature is not in complete harmony with that which you wish to achieve. Although my first experience with this phenomenon occurred while calling upon the name of El Shaddai, I have reproduced the exact same results by calling upon Vishnu, Baphomet, Sat Nam, Set, and Algol, the only alteration in the phenomenon being the entities that manifest. What *is* necessary is the undivided knowledge that this entity exists, not as some representation of your own splintered mind or chained psyche, but as an intelligent, corporeal being whose power is beyond limitation and whose ability to intervene in the very fabric of reality is undisputed, as well as having established a connection with that deity through the types of devices described in the first principle of evocation, which is preparatory immersion.

Employ all of the ritual devices as usual, paying special attention to the incense smoke, which should flood the Temple entirely, and the use of many candles, the color of which is to coincide with the nature of the deity to which you will offer your orations. In my spontaneous evocation of angelic legions, the mist from the quickly evaporating water, which in the southwest is often visible and most certainly a substantial vapor, very well could have taken the place of the incense smoke.

Most grimoires offer orations that can be used as presented or can be easily adapted to the specific deity that you will be invoking. The orison given in the eleventh chapter of the third book of The Book of the Sacred Magick of Abramelin the Mage[1] is an excellent example, although it most definitely does rely on the tenants of Judaism in its characteristics. In actuality, an unwritten, unrehearsed invocation, spoken in the rapture of the Divine is the most potent prayer for this evocation. Perhaps the greatest lesson learned within the halls of the Sacred Order of the Son of God is the act of humbling the ego and opening the human vessel to the inspirations and movements of the Divine, rather than relying on the imperfect mind of man for guidance – becoming a mouthpiece for god, the enactor of His will and word. By shutting down the mind, realizing that it is weak and fallible, accepting a source of knowledge that is both outside of ourselves and perfect, and acting and speaking as directed by the "Spirit," our words and acts are equally perfect. The result is spontaneous rather than forced. The universe moves in accordance with its nature, rather than against it. The words do not come from the human mind, but from the omniscience that possesses all. The power behind the words is then not that of human strength, but is the strength of the gods.

The whole process of this type of evocation, as well as the immediate result of the materialization of the spirits, is entirely spontaneous, and is difficult, if not impossible to control. It is also extraordinarily dependant on the ability of the Operator to manifest in this world that which he desires to see and to have. The deities who are elicited will respond, but the nature of the response may not be that which is sought if the Sorcerer has not prepared himself through practical occult experience and personal knowledge of the deity invoked through devotion or at least psychological and spiritual immersion in the characteristics and being of that deity. For this reason, only the Evocator who has successfully employed and Mastered every method of evocation given in this book thus far should attempt evocation of legions through faithful oration. Likewise, in the same manner in which the results of this evocation are completely spontaneous, the performance of the ritual itself should be spontaneous, as if the Evocator is called by the deity with which he has aligned himself to summon the entities that will do his will.

Chapter Ten
Evoking Without Bounds

The story cited in the latter part of the previous chapter recalled a time when I summoned into physical materialization legions of ministering angels through a powerful and faith-driven prayer. The whole Operation was entirely spontaneous, and utilized virtually none of the ritual devices used thus far, while still managing to adhere to the basic principles of evocation. As my Path diverted from that Sacred Order and I became more actively involved in the Ordo Ascensum Aetyrnalis in leadership roles, I noticed that full ritual with all of its tools and devices increasingly became a pretty novelty which neither aided nor impaired my ability to alter my reality through pure will. The moment in ritual when my desire took winged form and flew into the stratosphere to observe the world and to mold the changes that I had commanded had become so familiar to me that that moment could be duplicated instantaneously.

With that ability, I started to remove the devices which I once had so diligently applied in evocation, knowing by the examples of spontaneous evocation that I had experienced in my own life, such as the one cited above, that the ritual devices *could* indeed be taken away and the ritual would have the same if not a greater level of internal materialization and aftereffect as with them. The spirits themselves did not care whether the Circle is immaculately drawn, or if the wand perfectly flashes with yellow and red. The ritual devices create a Magickal dynamic that *is* most surely necessary. That dynamic, however, can be produced without the crutches. Again, the key to achieving this is to gain complete familiarity with the moment

173

of metaphysical activation, when that which was physical suddenly is transmuted into something beyond. Once the feeling and sensation of this moment is as familiar as the childhood rush of coming into the living room on Christmas morning to see the presents and the stockings, the emotions and sensations of which can be easily conjured even in the heat and the dryness of July, the Operator can begin to experiment in an attempt to discover the purpose of the metaphysical dynamic and the means by which it can be reproduced non-ritually if necessary.

As an example, the first item that you may wish to remove from ritual is any daggers, wands, staffs, or other will-projecting devices. In using them, you have sensed a rising up of energy and Magickal electricity within yourself, which moves into your chest, down your arm, through your hand, into the dagger, and leaves your immediate physical body through the blade, the energy then imparting into whatever external device was intended. Imagine the sensation of the travel of energy and power rising up within you and then traveling through you. Sense the moment that it leaves your body and moves towards the object. In ritual, why could you not simply use your fingers to move the energy where you wanted it to go? In actuality, since we are dealing with and energy and power that is not of this plane, why would it matter at all if your physical body made any motion towards any place? In the realms of spirit, every point is connected to every other point – there is no space between. The object that you wish to infuse with power is not over there, but it is in the same space that you inhabit. On the physical plane, these are separate spaces, but we are working upon this plane, not within it. If we relied on the physical world and its components to work our Magick, it would not be Magick at all, but simple labor. The energy does not need a dagger or a physical hand to tell it where to go. Rather, the pointing of the dagger and the motion of the hand tells the conscious mind where the energy should go, which then reaches into the will and directs the energy. Keeping your hands upon the altar and the dagger in your drawer, recreating the sensation of the moment when the energy moves from your body into the object, the tool, the physical limbs, and even the necessity of the transfer from the conscious mind is bypassed, allowing you to reach into pure will to cause change. Simply allow the energy to flow from you into the Circle around you, tracing the lines of the Triangle, moving into the brass of the chalice or the grains of the altar, by reproducing the sensation with which you have become familiar through doing so a hundred times with the proper orthodox tools. Do not altar the order in which the other ritual devices are charged, nor the intensity or saturation of the energy, but simply the vehicle by which the energy is moved.

The exact same process can be used for the chalice as well, its main use in ritual being the holding of the Elixir of Life which reinvests in the Operator the power of the Divine when the liquid is taken in. Does the Divine rest inside of wine? In ritual, omnipotence must be channeled into the fluid, which is then channeled back into the Operator at the given time. Instead, the effect can be reproduced without the wine and without the chalice, simply drinking the Blood of God in its pure form, without a liquid vehicle, simply drinking in through the soul the omnipotence of the Divine.

The altar, serving quite a practical purpose, should be kept in place. The consecration of it, however, can be just as automatic as the transfer of energy from the individual to the Circle or Triangle. In all cases, however, incantation and oration should be employed as before for remaining ritual implements. The speaking of the will in words that are direct and with purpose that is inarguable connects the physical to the spiritual, the spiritual to the physical, and all things to the desired end result.

The Temple of Manifestation

So far the Triangle of Manifestation has been used to designate the one place where the spirit should manifest, aside from those exercises in evoking legions into materialization. The traditional thought is that the Triangle serves as a type of astral prison for the spirit, keeping it bound within the Circle in the center of the Triangle, also kept inside through the runes or Tetragrammaton inscribed between the inner circle and the lines of the Triangle, forming a threefold protection against rebellious spirits. This originates from the belief that the spirits with which the Magician will work are by nature malevolent towards the Operator and his goals. This also assumes that the only power that the Operator can employ in the ritual of evocation is that of the Judaic god, and the only spirits that will answer the conjuration are those of

E.A. Koetting

demonic nature.   This archaic belief has been demolished by the Operations of thousands of Evocators through time. Not only can angels, elementals, planetary spirits, as well as countless other types of spirits who have no connection whatsoever to the Judaic or Christian be summoned to physical manifestation, the ritual may proceed without any reference to the name of God, the supposed Messiah, the Holy Spirit, or any of the saints. The power by which we Operate transcends the gods of any religion or the devices of any paradigm. The currents of Magick will affect reality regardless.

"…for He maketh this sun to rise on the evil and on the good, and sendeth rain on the just and on the unjust."[1]

In the Operations given in this text, the Triangle has been used to simply set apart a place for the spirit to materialize. It once again gives the conscious mind a place to direct the will to direct itself. If the Operator were to begin his first evocations without a Triangle, the conscious mind would experience great difficulty in not only directing the currents of the ritual altogether, but also in discerning the events taking place within the Temple. The mind of the Neophyte is unequipped to analyze and interpret those things whose origin is not this earth, and so it is a building process by which he is first able to see and to hear the spirits and to bring them into physical materialization. The mind, in this training process, needs a focal point, which is obscured more and more as he progresses and performs more difficult evocations, such as multiple evocations or the rites of evoking legions.

Once entire armies of entities have stood in the Temple, taking their places as they see fit, it should be no task to summon a single spirit and have it do the same. The Temple itself becomes the manifestation base, rather than the Triangle.   The spirit will materialize where it will, and will be freed to assume wondrous and terrible shapes if it chooses, and will also be able to produce visions and phenomenon that may definitely assist in the knowledge that may be requested by the Evocator.

Setting up the Temple with an altar and a Circle, and consecrating these through the projection of pure will, the evocation may proceed without the use of a Triangle. The entire room should be flooded with incense smoke, and alit with candle light. In such a free ritual, the manifestation of the spirit will take a more spontaneous form. Often, the white mist, which serves as a precursor to the full physical materialization of the spirit, will begin to gather in one spot, and then will seem to be instantly transported to another spot. The spirit, while manifesting, will shift locations in the Temple sporadically, seeming to jump from one place to another, struggling to enter this world, not yet confined by its spatial and temporal requirements, but still feeling its way around. Finally, it will materialize fully, often in a form that is much more vivid and unrestrained than ever before. Its voice usually has more clarity and depth than any spirit previously, and the whole image of the thing will be much more stark and intimidating. The spirit will walk in this world without boundaries, pacing the Temple if it so desires, or even causing its familiars to manifest with it. All bounds are removed from the spirit's abilities for materialization, and the ritual will likewise bear fruit without bounds.

Breaking the Circle

The primary rule for the performance of any ritual, especially one as volatile and sensitive as evocation to physical manifestation, is that a Circle is to always be drawn on the ground, and that until the spirit is dismissed and possibly banished, the Circle is never to be broken. The Magick Circle forms the only barrier between the Magician and his subject, between the physical world and the waiting abyss, and also between man and his limitless nature. While the Circle also represents eternity and the great loop of timelessness, it is bound. Limitlessness would possibly be better represented with a one-dimensional dot in the center of the Temple, or even better, with nothing at all.

The published and highly fictionalized accounts of nearly occultists who have in some way accidentally broken the Circle during evocation usually conclude with diagnoses of insanity or death of one or all of the Circle's occupants. There is an unpublished number, as well as a minority of published occultists, however, whose breaking of the Circle was far from accidental, and who have resultantly discovered a new intercourse with the spirits that they summon. A few years ago I set out to find those who have crossed the boundaries of sanity and safety established by millennia of religious and metaphysical practice, and have held lengthy conversation with them concerning their methods and the results. It has since been a sobering thing to recollect those conversations and to discover the similarities between our experiences, both with the ritual, and afterwards in our daily lives.

As one gentleman put it, "We haven't just reached a new level with these experiments; we aren't even playing the same game anymore."

Performing an evocation without a Circle right away would indeed be foolish, and death or madness may very well be guaranteed as the warnings of the ancients imply. Evocation summons up in the human being psychological forces that are by nature dangerous, but also summons up into this world from one far beyond real entities who carry with them power that the flesh and the mind are weak to withstand. The awesome power of evocation is also its inherent danger. The Sorcerer must therefore wade slowly into the black waters of the abyss until he is not aware that he can no longer breathe.

Perform the ritual of evocation employing the Triangle and the Circle as is given in Chapter Five. In this particular ritual, the Circle should be drawn on the ground lightly, while the construction of the Triangle is to be more durable. When the spirit has arrived and is fully materialized within the Triangle, brush the lines of the Circle nearest the Triangle with your hand, completely erasing them from sight. Sense the Magical protection of the Circle dissipating as you do so. You now are supposedly unprotected from whatever malice the spirit may wish upon you, save for that granted by the Triangle. Unless you consider yourself to be a righteous Practitioner, using your power only for altruistic, godly works, and you are attempting in this ritual to summon, constrain, and command a demon by the words and names of some polarized god or another, you will likely notice that the spirit summoned does not react to the breaking of the Circle. You will notice that it does not attempt to raise chains and rivets from Hell to bring you under, nor does it attempt to draw lightning from the sky to strike you down. It instead waits to be greeted and to commence with the Working. The Magickal protection granted to the Sorcerer does not come from a drawn or imagined symbol on the ground or in the air, but has its origin from within, from the very godlike nature of the Operator.

Interesting to note is the adage that it is not possession or physical harm that is most dangerous when dealing with spirits, but instead is *obsession* – being drawn to a particular spirit or type of spirit beyond the point of reason and objectivity. The closer to the physical plane and the Magician's Temple that a spirit is drawn, the closer they are brought into his or her "sphere of influence," where vague and invisible connections and communications can take place, often without the knowledge of the human communicator. The great danger in performing these rituals of evocation without the established boundaries does not come from the spirits at all, but from the Evocators. If the Circle is broken with trembling hands and hearts racing with the expectation of harm, the spirit will answer that call, and will deliver. If the Magician anticipates a black gulf to swallow him up once he has crossed the boundaries of the Circle, that abyss will rise up in that same instant. If, instead, the Adept crosses these boundaries with the sure knowledge that in doing so, he is erasing boundaries altogether and entering a new stage of his evolution, that step will be his first into the Limitless.

After having performed at least three evocations in the above manner, relying at first upon the presence of the Triangle and the Circle for initial protection, enter the Temple again and draw the Circle on the ground, omitting the Triangle. The evocation will proceed as given earlier in this chapter, and the Temple will fill with spiritual chaos as the entity materializes. It is into this chaos that you must step. With the spirit standing before you, unbound by any Triangle and waiting to be greeted, step over the boundaries of the Circle, leaving the lines of visibly intact, and meet the spirit in the open space of the Temple.

It is unusual for this first face-to-face encounter to be entirely lucid. The overwhelming spiritual fatigue incurred by the simple action of disposing of boundaries between the Operator and the subject will easily threaten the conscious state of the Evocator. The mind will no longer be able to compartmentalize the ritual and tell the lie that concrete reality is within the Circle whereas "subjective reality" is within the Triangle. The mind is forced to deny reality as determined by social programming in combination with expectation based on past experience, or to quit its job altogether. Often, the mind chooses the latter approach, and the Magician is left to either collapse under the weight of the heavens or the underworld embodied before him, or to switch to that intelligence and mind which does not originate in the dying and fallible brain. Either way, however, the experience of the evocation and its particulars are uniquely difficult to recall after the fact, and the Adept is prone to not speak, write, draw, or otherwise communicate it for utter lack of ability. The Masters spend a good deal of their time in silence on purpose.

Like killing or making love, evoking to this degree of intimate, unrestrained interaction requires repetition before the experience can be integrated and can be assigned any particular value. The initial act serves as an initiation into Godhood, a breaking of the conventions that once kept you safe, but now keep you imprisoned. It is an act of defiance to the laws that supposedly bind, and an affirmation of autonomy. The second repetition serves as a confirmation of your autonomous reign, and of your determination to press forward towards your limitless nature. It is in the third and all subsequent repetitions that all of this is forgotten and that the experience can be integrated and can truly impress you at a deep level, rather than just scathing the surface. It is also beyond the third repetition that the drug of power becomes addictive.

In most cases, this three-step rise into godhood or fall from grace applies to the three types of Practitioners above: killers, lovers, and ritual Magicians.

The final step away from the binds that you have given yourself is to evoke to full manifestation any entity of your choosing, without a Circle or a Triangle, from the start of the ritual to its conclusion. Remove yourself to a remote location, preferably in open space. Living in the southwest United States, I would likely drive through the desert on a dirt road until the sights and sounds of the cities disappeared, and then I might go even further by walking for fifteen minutes or more away from the road.

Set the sigil of the spirit on the ground, and make a small fire in the direction in which the spirit's nature dictates that it will appear. For safety reasons, the fire should be enclosed in a pit, which should be no more than twelve inches in diameter. Have on hand a good deal of dried Dittany of Crete leaves or sage leaves, which you will use as your incense.

Sit in meditation upon the ritual, the spirit, and the end result that you are manifesting through the evocation. Invoke omnipotence and sense the same power, which has entered into you in every evocation ritual in the past, enter now. Drop a good amount of leaves on the fire, near to the point of smothering it, creating a thick smoke that will permeate the air around you.

Turn the sigil face up and gaze into it, establishing the connection with the spirit, linking your mind to its mind, your energy to its energy, your power to its power. Feel the spirit being drawn to you, to your desert place, to the smoke of the fire and to the realm of the flesh. Call out, "(Spirit's name), hear my voice, see my signs, and know that I command creation to bring you before me, so that I may see you, so that I may hear you, and so that your power will be my power, your strength will be my strength, and your knowledge will be my knowledge." Touch the face of the spirit's sigil, imparting all power and filling the fibers of the paper with light, and say, "I seal this calling upon you, and so you shall rise!"

The spirit will rise, and will face you as one man faces another, and will speak to you as one man to another. But those who have been forever branded by this type of evocation are those who the spirit has touched once it has been summoned to take form before them, for the spirit does not touch as one man might touch another. The spirit's fingers do not stop at the skin, but penetrate gently past the muscle and the bone. The spirit's mind is not bound to the brain, but flows through its every limb equally, and its power does not need to be gathered, for it possesses it in full always, and at that touch which goes within, all of these things will pass into the Master, and for a moment he will not be human, but will become that spirit – will become undying, powerful without limit, and for one moment the whole of his existence will serve a single, pointed purpose. While the touch of the spirit may be felt by the nerves in the hand, on the shoulder, or as brush on the cheek, the soul is drawn out by the contact, and in that instant something from beyond is drawn in.

Chapter Eleven

Summoning God

There are no bounds with the power We bring. All spirits may be summoned forth by any of the methods given above, in any context that will lead to the growth, development, enrichment, and constant Ascent of the Evocator. Legions may be called forth from heaven or from hell and be brought under your command, to sweep through the cities and over the earth and even across oceans to bring to pass that which you have willed. Beautiful and garish rituals may be used to bring the invisible into sight, or they may simply be called to commune with the Conjurer through the power and potency inherent in man through his unconquerable nature. The seraphim and the jinn, the intelligences and the shells, the demons and the deceased will all rise when they are called by the Sorcerer who has armed himself with this secret knowledge and has fortified himself with the experience of its application. All needful things may be brought to his door or laid upon his hearth, and all that he might desire to know or to have is within his ability to summon. All that remains is to summon the Gods.

Looking back at the metaphor that was drawn with all of existence being a machine, every entity within it being the wheels, cogs, and springs which make the machine move, and the Maker himself being inserted into the machine in the form of human beings, it must be clear that ALL embodiments aside from man serve a limited function and are given limited power to carry out that function. The Divine Soul, however, has no real limitations, but only perceived weaknesses. If the perception of a particular Magician dictates that he can summon angelic entities galore without incident, but that in the instant of attempting to summon a demon he will be devoured by the flames of Hell, he is not likely to have success in demonic evocation. Beginning from a fresh slate wherein the Sorcerer is able to summon naturally non-resistant entities such as elementals or planetary familiars and eventually move on to the dignitaries of the elements and the Sephirotic angels, summoning any demon or archangel or those entities who have no title or description but who come when power is called will be no more difficult for the experienced Evocator than was the first evocation of an elemental spirit. Indeed, legions of these beings can be evoked to physical materialization with nothing more than a greater degree of dedication to the Working and an understanding of and preparedness for the forces and currents that would otherwise devastate his psyche and his physical health as well. This same structure applies to all forms of evocation, even when the entity to be evoked is a Godform.

With these things taken into consideration, the only two obstacles to the successful evocation of any Godform to physical materialization are the perceptions, attachments, and fears of the Evocator, and the stamina of the essential elements of the physical world in withstanding the immeasurable force of the God setting literal foot on this dusty ground.

The ancient grimoires warn of worldwide cataclysm and decisive deaths of Jupiterian figures resulting from the evocation of a god. The whole of the lower worlds will revolt at its presence, and earthquakes, floods, hurricanes, fires, and mobs will follow. There are few, if any measures that can ensure safety after such an evocation. It is this aspect of evoking godforms that demands discipleship and spiritual union with the god to be summoned before the evocation takes place. The principle of preparatory immersion here is fulfilled through devotion.

The first level of devotion is intellectual. Before any adult freely decides to alter his lifestyle in subjection to an ideal or archetype, he or she will often spend a great amount of time studying the dictates, disciplines, habits, and tenets of the new lifestyle, upon which they will base their decision to flee from it, or they will be drawn even deeper into its chasms. In devoting yourself to the god or goddess that you wish to summon, you should commence a thorough study of it, ciphering through the texts that declare the nature and the personality of the deity. You will most benefit from your intellectual pursuit in returning to the most ancient sources, those cultures who first received spiritual transmissions from the god.

The second level of devotion is devotion itself. The task for the Evocator is to dedicate every minute of every day to the deity, and to fill his every action and word with purpose leading to communion with it. If a certain color is attributed to the god you have chosen, that color should be worn as often as possible, or some tangible element relating to the deity can be carried in a pocket or purse.

Choose a day and an hour appropriate for the Summoning of your God, giving yourself at least thirteen days of devotion beforehand. In the morning of every day, you are to enter your Temple or simply clear a space in an unoccupied room, and kneel like a Christian or a Muslim in prayer. Give your oration in the same manner as instructed in the previous chapter, not regurgitating memorized words but allowing the "spirit" or essence of your god fill you and speak through you. In doing so, the deity is in a way addressing itself, calling itself into your life, rather than a mere man attempting to command a god. In your oration, consecrate your day and all of its activities to your deity. As the oration commences, sense the essence of your god entering the Temple, filling its fibers and bringing all things around you into recognition of Its majesty. Allow your spiritual sight to open at least enough to view and to become aware of the powerful currents flowing around you. Your god will not take embodied form at this point, but will condense its permanent omnipresence enough to form an engulfing radiance in the Temple. Depending on which deity you have chosen to evoke, the air will grow thicker or will thin as It manifests, the light will brighten or dim, or perhaps the room will become hotter, colder, damper, or barren. The invocation will take an undeniable form, at which point you may cease your praying and put your attention on the presence of your god.

The presence of your god, summoned into the Temple through your orations, needs to be brought into critical mass in order to have a lasting effect on you, on your life, and in your world. Through the calling of Its name, the deity will hear you, and will answer. Through the prayer, it will draw near to you. But it is through complete transformation of the self that it is brought *forth*. In the final chapter of the book <u>Works of Darkness</u>, a formula is given which solidifies the presence of the deity to a real and lasting degree. The word "solidify" is used here rather than "materialize," as the deity is not at this phase constructing a condensed, corporeal form in which It will manifest to you, the Operator, but is instead bringing Its omniscient presence which is scattered throughout existence and focusing it entirely on the Temple, and on the Sorcerer, taking a nebulous force and giving it substance.

The exact method given for producing this result, following the previous devotions offered, is the use of an incantation which could be likened unto a sutra, but is more closely akin to the short of rations called Enns, discussed previously in this text. The incantation given here was passed to me through an occult transmission from specific entities that exist outside of any identifying classification given here or in any other text, but who, because of their absolute fiery nature, would often be considered "demonic" or infernal by the educated onlooker. The language of the incantation is one that is used throughout my writings and my Workings, and has proven to not only be a concise, albeit largely untranslatable language, but also to possess a raw Magickal potency beyond any other spoken Enn or sutra I have come across thus far in my own journey of Ascent. It is to be given in a clear yet calm tone, the words should be spoken in rapid succession without smearing the beginning of one word into the ending of the previous. Each repetition should also follow the previous as well, allowing you enough time to take a breath and begin again. The incantation will then take on sing-songish rhythm, and the tempo will naturally increase with each repetition. The first few repetitions unite the mind with the currents of the incantation, allowing the psyche to assimilate the alien tongue and to begin to transfer the energy and power from it into the Being. It is usually after the third recital of the incantation that it will begin to manifest change.

As given in <u>Works of Darkness</u>:

"As you continue to give the oration, the mind and body will ascend towards the upper stratosphere of the soul and will begin to reap the rewards of the power that is being called. As this moment of Union draws near, a unique state of rapture will begin to build within you, the incantation moving forward in a frenzied haste to clutch Eternity and devour it whole. The brain will tire of the redundant phrase and will cease to pay it any attention, allowing the remainder of the Self to continue without its interference. You may find that the repetitious words of the invocation begin to muddle, some being transposed, some being misspoken or left out altogether while other words may even be replaced with new ones, fresh words that ring of the same alienic vibration, yet never were before seen in writing or heard in speech. The repetitions will increase in speed and fervor exponentially until each word melts with the ones before and after it, and the entire phrase disappears, yet the Being, the Self, still buzzes with the electricity of it. It is as if the incantation has reached the critical mass that is the single necessary component in this Operation and exists independent of the will of the Operator. The incantation continues to repeat itself in the air of the Temple, heard by the Magician and his God alone.[1]

Having prepared yourself through meditation and through open invocation to your god, give now the following incantation, which will call that force which circles the Temple into manifestation:

Teat astru malku N.
Seine astru maella treine N.
Altu sentu estru N.
Ecks entru antra N.
N. astru teat N.

As the incantation is repeated and begins to incite ecstasy and frenzy, the presence of your God will begin to thicken in the Temple. Often, this will be accompanied by mental flashes of visions and voices, transmissions of your own from that deity whom you call. When the verbal proclamation of the incantations fades into silence, you will find yourself enveloped in the bliss of your God, surrounded and impaled by It. It is not unusual at this point for the disciple to enter into a spiritual and psychological state that produces glossolalia, known more popularly as the "gift of tongues." Such a state of rapture and the resulting temporary dementia involved will work to rid you of your mind altogether, leaving your Higher Understanding to receive further transmissions from the deity and also to transmit through that state to the remainder of existence. Like the voodoo practitioners, the tribal sorcerers, or the Pentecostals who experience similar, albeit more erratic and less focused forms of this state, you may find yourself convulsing on your Temple floor, stammering the name of your God.

While the above is an extreme manifestation of the presence of the deity, a less intense reaction does not necessarily denote a lesser manifestation. The vital aspect here is an unspoken communion with your God. Once that communion has been achieved, your day may begin with God in your heart.

This daily devotion and communion should be held as the first and last activity of your day, being performed upon waking and before returning to sleep.

The third level of devotion is association. Either during the thirteen day devotion given above, or after the thirteen days have passed, evoke one entity that is subservient to your deity each day, questioning them concerning the deity Itself and the ritual by which you may evoke It. Initially, the spirits will be wary of granting you this information, especially concerning the ritual of evocation, but with prompting and steadfastness, they will submit to your wishes. Along with information about the deity and the consequences of evoking It, each entity will give you a piece of the puzzle which will allow you to summon your god to full materialization, and you might also find the details that they give towards the nature of the deity to be rather intimate, and will most definitely aid in your ability to create and sustain a substantial contact with It.

The spirits, especially those who serve the deity in the closest proximities, will guide you in procuring or constructing a symbol or device through which such necessary substantial contact may be made, as ordinary sigils will not suffice, nor will the metals and the incenses that would normally bring any spirit into manifestation. These ritual devices are specific to each god, and will need to be explained in detail by the spiritual servant of that god. Often, as explained below, the incense used is the heat of fresh blood, and the symbol of connection might be drawn on the ground spanning yards of earth, or might be carved or imprinted on the skin of the Operator. These are the details that must be discovered through these preparatory evocations.

The fourth level of devotion is preparation. It is in this step that the basic preparations for the ritual of evocation are made, in accordance with the guidance given by the emissaries of the deity that you have evoked. There may be times, more often than not, that these preparations will take days or weeks for the procuring of specific elements of the ritual, or for any additional personal preparations which you have been guided in. The gods, through the mouths of their angels, their demons, or their spirits, do indeed demand much from those who would request Their personal and physical attendance, and these demands must be met without fail. There is an inherent danger and fatal risk in even the most simple forms of evocation, and this is only multiplied when attempting to summon forth a being whose power can cause the oceans to drown the highest mountains. Only great care in adhering to the instructions that you are given will temper the walls of your Temple and the cells of your body to withstand the inferno when the God returns.

The fifth level of devotion is sacrifice. All things that are enduring must be seeded in blood. Every great empire has built its first foundations on tremendous and usually bloody sacrifice. A god is never evoked to run some simple errand or to do some Magickal favor, but is summoned forth to make a lasting change in the world, to herald in a new Aeon, and to bring about the apocalyptic final harvest, which allows Eden to blossom once more.

The Gods demand sacrifices, and these must be met in order to bring them into manifestation. While in prayer They may be invoked, and in ritual Their names and powers may be called to imbue some goal with Their force, it is only through the levels of devotion outlined above, and the final devotion of sacrifice that They will appear in physical form to speak to Their disciples as one man speaks to another. There is no great formula for the evocation of a God aside from this.

Throughout the Evocator's career he or she may very well have discovered the importance of blood or some other living sacrifice to provide for the most stable and sure materialization of the spirit, as well as for the absolute achievement of his or her will. A supreme sacrifice must be made, however, for the evocation to physical materialization of a God. The exact nature of this sacrifice is made known to the Adept in the process of summoning the spirits serving that god, and in the invocations that precede the Working.

The esoteric Order to which I have sworn myself challenges its adherents through lessons tailored to the spiritual, emotional, and psychological needs of its members. As the Chela progresses through the lessons, they become more challenging and require more intrinsic abilities to successfully complete each lesson. As the student nears the eighteenth and final initiation, each lesson is not only more difficult, but also may take months or even years to complete rather than hours or days.

On the eighteenth of December, 2002, I received the initial instructions for the receipt of the seventeenth initiation: to evoke to physical manifestation a specific God, whose name and attributes I have been sworn to not reveal, but have always referred to even in my own journals as D. In the evening of the following day, I received more details concerning this evocation, being given by my mentor the same instructions that I have recorded in this chapter. My invocations revealed the details of the plot – the evocation needed to take place outside, yet to be contained within rock walls with no ceiling and a very large headway, I was instructed in an exact method of assumption of omnipotence, and I was given the formula for the manifestation base, which I have since found to be the most potent base for materialization of spirits. No sigil was to be used, and instead the name of D. would be the tool to link myself with Him.

The night of the evocation bore a full moon, and a thin mist draped the small southwest town in an unusual, if not unheard of gesture, creating a halo around the moon at least four times its apparent size. I remember a crackling silence that night as well, and feeling as if my incantations would ring through the air with a crisp tone that would carry into the ears of all of the sleeping. An abandoned racquetball court sitting on the same lot as one of the county's oldest and most unused cemeteries provided a perfect Temple for the Working – a large, square, cinderblock room rising up two stories with the ceiling open to the sky, which provided a view of the looming moon at the exact hour chosen for the evocation. I gathered the implements and procured the sacrifice as instructed, and made my way through the dark night and the floating mist towards the Temple court.

Sweeping the cracked and weathered concrete clean, I sat in meditation, mostly to gather myself internally before proceeding with the immense. With a thick stick of white chalk, I drew the Circle as D.'s angels had taught me to, and to the outside of it in the west I drew a smaller circle with three alien characters marking the vertices of an invisible Triangle. The chalice was placed within the smaller circle, into which I poured and dropped and squeezed the components of my manifestation base, which by the aroma and the fumes of decomposition created effluvia capable of giving rise to a spirit body without the use of fire or smoke.

I fortified the implements through incantations and visualizations specific to the evocation, and in the center of the Circle I offered the sacrifice as I was instructed, adding the blood of it to the manifestation base in the chalice. I began the orations and could instantly sense D.'s presence drawing near; much nearer and much more quickly than that with which I was comfortable. Almost immediately after reciting what could normally be called the "conjuration," dark fumes began to visibly rise from the chalice, and the body of my God started to form before me.

I was terrified and wordless in the moment that He materialized, a gigantic figure cloaked in shadows, His body appearing to reach most of the height of the room, His eyes changing from a burning red to an unearthly green, and his voice seeming to thunder from his chest rather than his mouth.

Having forgotten the salutation that I had carefully and diligently committed to memory in the instant of His appearance, and even seeming to forget the whole purpose of the evocation altogether at His sight, I blunderingly proclaimed, "D., give to me all of your power," in the most self-sure tone that I could muster, feeling like an ant with a breadcrumb staring up at the foot that is about to crush it.

D. laughed, not mockingly as I had expected, but instead a jovial laugh quite contrary to His dreadful manifestation, and He did not crush me with his foot, but instead replied, "You already have it!" He began to guide me, as a patient teacher might with a grade-school student, in many ways that I might be able to access these powers which I supposedly possessed, mainly through the manipulation of my subtle bodies, maintaining throughout that the only limitation put on my abilities and on the power that I sought have been put in place by my own self.

After a term of this instruction, D. reached His hand out, passing it over the lines of Circle, and asked if I would come with Him. I recognized the implicit request to leave my body to do so, and my mind raced with fear and doubt. Was this God who I had worshipped, and also who terrified me, setting a trap for my demise? Was He drawing me out of the Circle to leave me for dead at the hands of His demons, or to fling my soul into a hell created specifically for the naïve? He did not urge, but waited patiently with his hand out, and I could not decline. I rose from my body through the opening above and rather than finding myself looking down upon the city, instead found myself looking down on creation. D. stood beside me, His image entirely different, now appearing to be an entity of immeasurable size and power, not confined to a material body, and no longer did I see darkness and fear when I looked upon Him, but complete splendor and true awe. I fell into worship of Him in that moment, and the awe has still not dimmed.

We looked down on creation, at all of the stars and the swirling galaxies, and D. stated, "All of these are yours, if you take them."

After instructing me through three-dimensional, first person visions in the method of precipitation of will, or as He termed it, "pure creation and destruction," D. returned me to my body, and I do not know if that body was already on the floor asleep, but if it was not it quickly became that way. The experience was more than my flesh could sustain, and I still uncover pieces of memory that have been lost when I returned from that journey.

D. was the first God that I had evoked, and I have since found no need for another. Through evocation, I had learned to control the flesh and the mind. Through evocation I had gained power over the earth and the elements. Through evocation I had commanded legions to war beside me. Through evocation I learned from a God that through these secret and forbidden arts I can become like He is, do all that He can do, and even greater things.

E.A. Koetting

LEILAH PUBLICATIONS

HTTP://LEILAH.ORG
FACEBOOK.COM/LEILAHPUBLICATIONS

CPSIA information can be obtained at www.ICGtesting.com
Printed in the USA
LVOW102355010313

322330LV00011B/524/P

9 780982 999240